THE RICHEST MERCHANT IN GREECE

By

Jerry Amwe

This page was intentionally left empty

The Richest Merchant in Greece

By Jerry Amwe

Contact author via: jerryamwe@gmail.com; +2348068743062

To publish and distribute this material in print please contact the author or amazon.com

@ copyright 2015. e-copy by Amazon kindle publisher and paper print by create space publishers

ASIN: B015A4NLWY

ISBN-13: 978-1517319502 (Create Space-Assigned)

ISBN-10: 1517319501

Book Cover design: Adedayo Ogunkeye: +2348096498194

The writings dates back to 506BC and beyond.

Staging: Ancient Athens, Greece

Reviews are greatly appreciated by the author

Dedication

To my Dad (Vincent D. Amwe), for all the years of fatherhood.

&

To all who aspire for abundance in life, and sought for the bliss of life.

Contents (Base on Chapters)

FOREWORD

THE RICHEST MERCHANT IN GREECE is a book project born not only out of the author's creative imagination but also from in dept research. When growing up, the author created an unique interest in reading ancient histories especially those of the Greeks, Jews, Babylonians, Egyptians, Romans, and others, he followed great figures of the past and their achievements and took the time to understand how wealth was made from the ancient times and with the help of books like *the richest man in Babylon* he was encouraged knowing that these ancient principles were the basis of our modern wealth. He discovered that these principles of wealth were timeless and could be applied in every generation to bridge the gap between the rich and the poor.

If you look at our world today, you will agree that the wealthiest of families on earth have had these game played well for centuries and handed over to them by their predecessors and also, ancient Greek philosophies, wisdom, government and traditions dominate a major part of our civilization, there are greater references to the Greek culture than any other, and for such reasons the author took an interest in finding how the Greeks accumulated wealth in time pass and to also understand the daily life of merchants and nobles of the past. This curiosity was what led to the writing of the book "THE RICHEST MERCHANT IN GREECE"

And the book title was so chosen in order to help readers relate it with already familiar books of ancient writings about wealth. It was challenging and time consuming compiling such a piece considering the lost histories of the past but the motivation to travel back to the lost past and bring forth something out of creative imagination to the future in order to help men and women succeed in life kept the author going. A huge credit is attributed great thinkers and writers whose ideas, stories, illustrations and writings were partly used to make this book worthwhile, the author will be grateful to receive words from readers and contributions for a profound updated edition. Our happiness will be complete should this book be able to help you appreciate the past and also attain the goal for which it was written.

From the Author

Jerry Amwe

jerryamwe@gmail.com

GET RICH, BE POWERFUL AND STAY HAPPY

"Many admire, few know"

Hippocrates (460-357BC)

THINK of the things money can do for you;

It can set you free, make possible your dreams and help you master earthly wants and possessions.

With money, a man can travel to distant lands and enjoy different cultures. He can be generous to friends and family, feed the needy, shelter the homeless and cloth the naked.

Money spices up love and relationships; with it, a man could buy the most expensive of fabric and ornaments of gold and silver for a damsel, and also build great mansions to his delight and bring to his table bountiful dishes, wines, spices, and sea foods from faraway lands.

He can build great temples and statues of his desire and make huge donations to the public; he can build charitable homes for orphans and widows and buy himself an army of war for protection.

A man could buy himself names, influence, positions, titles, fame, and fortunes of hidden riches.

Money makes your worship more comfortable because it answers almost all that you pray for and gives you a better reason to be grateful.

It is the most valuable medium of exchange on earth and the very substance by which earthly riches could be measured.

The man who acquires more of it, and can produce more of it, becomes the richest of his counterparts.

In all your getting, get wisdom and get riches!

INTRODUCTION

Greece: where slaves work to enrich masters

Greece, a society driven by slavery, was situated around the East Mediterranean. The Greeks used the sea to their advantage and maneuvered their way into greatness and prosperity. They became powerful by conquering other nations and taking away their riches. They drew the world to themselves and became the center for philosophy, art, architecture, science, politics, commerce, and religious obligations.

Athens, favorite city of the gods and center of greatness, ruled over Greece as the most powerful City and achieved so much with the help of her great leaders, thinkers, armies, merchants, and slaves. The Golden age brought Athens into light, the discovery of the silver mine and the victorious war against the Persians opened the boundaries of Athens to great prosperity and power. They had a lot of Slaves from wars and used them to build great temples and monuments unto their gods. The Acropolis stands out at the peak of Athens with great buildings like the Parthenon, the temple of Athena Nike and other master buildings. The Athenians so much believed in their gods that they made a magnificent statue of the goddess Athena whom they believed watches over Athens.

The land of Greece was surrounded by rocks so they could not farm and harvest much; they had to make trade with other Nations like the Egyptians, Phoenicians, Lydia and other Cities to meet their basic needs. They relied heavily on the man power of slaves to accomplish most of their task and Slaves were so much especially in Athens that their number almost outnumbered that of the citizens. Every street and home was filled with all kinds of Slaves: Household slaves, work slaves, entertainers, hetaeras (educated courtesans), and miners.

Although slaves were treated fairly in Athens, but they had no claims to property only a few exceptions; they could not bring a suit or serve as a defendant; they could not offer testimony except under torture. They had no legally recognized family relationships, lacked the public rights and duties of citizens, were restricted from many (but not all) religious festivals and played a small, but sometimes pivotal, role in the military. Moreover, a master could treat his slave as he wished but there were degrees to which slaves were whipped, fettered, tattooed and otherwise corporally violated.*

Pericles, the Athenian leader during the golden age tried to enlarge the wealth and power of Athens. He used the money from the Delian League's treasury to build Athens' 200-ship navy into the strongest in the Mediterranean. A strong navy was important" because it helped Athens strengthen the safety of its empire. Athenian prosperity depended on gaining access to its surrounding waterways. It needed overseas trade to obtain supplies of grain and other raw materials. Pericles had three goals in mind: First, to strengthen Athenian democracy; second, to hold and strengthen the empire and third, to glorify Athens.* He transformed Athens and made it a Jewel unto Greece through the construction of magnificent structures at the Acropolis of which the Parthenon was the most spectacular, he also gave the Sculptor Phidias to construct the glorious statue of the goddess Athena and this brought great glory to the Athenians.

It was during these times in Athens that Merchants also flourished greatly but some Merchants grew richer than the others... And this was the case with THE RICHEST MERCHANT IN GREECE

*Sale for the purpose of freedom: slave-prostitutes and manumission in ancient Greece, DEBORAH KAMEN
* Democracy and Greece golden age

GET RICH

CHAPTER

1

THE RICHEST MERCHANT IN GREECE

All men were created equal but a few decide to become rich.

N oises from traders filled the atmosphere.

The place was very crowded with all class of people trying to buy and sell, from the wine stands to the fabric merchants at extreme end of the market were displayed exotic spices from distant lands, jewelries, perfumes, linen, Ornaments, fruits, beef, grains, and all sorts of household articles for sale. Slaves carried about goods for their masters and courtesans hanged by the corners waiting for clients to ease their sexual urge, craftsmen were under the heat of the day working and making tools of different varieties and politicians were at a distance discussing issues about the state of Athens. The Agora (market place) was the heart of Athens where commerce, politics, and cultural activities took place.

Monopoly

In one of the houses of the Agora, Merchants from different parts of Greece gathered and began discussing amidst themselves, it was like a symposium with wines and different delicacies offered to them as they discussed. But Most of them cared less of what was before them; they were more concerned of the anguish within their hearts as they talked in bitter voices with one another:

"Why should only one man acquire so much wealth for himself? This is not fair!" said a merchant "we all work together under the same sun but in just few years, he had grow n so wealthy than all of us combined, why should life be so unfair to us?" spoke the Jewel Merchant. "It is true my fell ow Merchants, he has spoken rightly, if we do not find out the secret behind his wealth, we shall soon lose our profits to him and have nothing to feed ourselves. He has domina ted every street in Athens and almost all the wealthiest me n in Athens patronize him far more than any of us here." P atios the Artisan spoke.

AND ANTONIO THE POTER CHIPED IN, "Could it be that he uses dark powers to make riches? And even if he practices sorcery we should have known, because most of us here h ave one time or the other visited almost all of the sorcerer s in Athens in search of fortune and they cannot make a m an this rich without a form of torment added to his life. Bu t he has accumulated riches in different ways, enjoys the b est of life and is very generous, we see how he dresses his slaves in silk clothing and treats them as free men, I sugges t we call upon him so we can ask of him to understand our plight as fellow merchants, and perhaps reveal to us whate ver he uses to accumulate such wealth, he should please gi ve us a part of this secret portion so we can prosper and n ot perish in our wants".

"O! Brothers, come to your senses, why do you talk like fo ols, who is that man on the surface of the earth that would reveal his secret of prosperity to you that you may grow w ealthier than him? Be wise, such a man does not exist; he will rather choose to die with his secrets than reveal them to you because a man is as powerful as to the degree of se crets he can withhold within him for it is these secrets that gives him the advantages to rule and dominate others. I believe Rich Basileus will not reveal anything of significance to you how much more his secrets of prosperity, moreover, he is now THE RICHEST MERCHANT IN GREECE, and I do not think he will desire another man to take such an enviable title away from him" said Lycus the Chief Merchant of the Agora.

HMMM...TRUE YOUR LORDSHIP, WE NEVER THOUGHT THIS DEEP, they all nodded in agreement.

The Decision

ANTONIO after a deep thought spoke out, "Well, my Lord and fellow merchants, it seems I may deviate from your thoughts for I do not agree to what you say, we should not conclude so easily without hearing from him first. If he chooses not to reveal to us the secrets to his riches then we can find other ways to help ourselves"

AND SOME OF THE MERCHANTS AGREED WITH Antonio, but there erupt a great division amidst them and most went with Lycus, for he was a prominent and influential merchant in Athens.

And Lycus spoke up again, "Well, you all can go ahead and seek after him in vain, as for me; I shall gather my wealth my own way for anyone reasonable enough will know the truth in what I say, for the man Basileus shall reveal nothing to you of significance"

And they left the Agora that day more confused and in division with just a few who agreed to see THE RICHEST MERCHANT IN GREECE.

CHAPTER

2

THE SECRET

"If you wish to know the road up the mountain, ask the per son who goes back and forth on it,"

Zerin

Basileus had grown very prosperous in Athens and has dominated most of Athenian commerce, he s upplies armors to the Athenian Armies, pottery to neighboring cities, silk to the prominent men in Greece, gr ains to Athenians, and all sort of spices and precious stone s to distant lands. He has ships that travel through the Me diterranean to purchase the best of ornaments, jewels, bla ck stones, and grains; He has gathered for himself an army of slaves and owns the finest of buildings, lands, entertain ers, and gardens in Athens. He mingles with the politicians and Philosophers of Athens and has loyal friends in high po sitions in the government. He takes counsel from the temp le Priest and watches his ways I order to deal fairly with all men and make peace with them.

The Plight for Riches

The merchants arrived at the enviable mansion f the Rich B asileus.

Basileus: "You are welcome my good friends, I received yo ur message from my servant and learnt you seek after me. I am pleased to have you here today, may I know to what honor I have your visit today? For I am delighted to have y ou under my roof"

Antonio: "It is true Rich Basileus that we seek after thee.

We have grown weary and frustrated of our trades, becaus
e we prosper less in them. It is obvious that you alone hav
e dominated the market and we live barely on the crumbs
of your table··· so, we have decided to seek after the secre
t of your prosperity that we may not perish in our lack"

Patios: "It is true my Lord, you have grown so rich and hav
e become THE RICHEST MERCHANT IN GREECE. Our wealth
combined cannot equal yours and you live a much lavished
life than us all, your wealth grows more as the days goes b
y, and it marvels us how a man can grow this rich in Athen
s that he controls almost all the trade and has great influe
nce in the politics of Athens. We desire to know thy secret
and the price we must pay to prosper like you"

Anakletos chipped in, "And also my Lord, you know how h
ard we do work under the sun and sometimes miss our fa
milies and friends on many voyages in search of riches, we
sought after money the best we can but when the money
comes, we cannot give an account on how it was spent, ou
r debts keeps growing by the day. We neither can give our
wives the best of treats nor our children the best of learnin
g and our wants in life keeps increasing by the day··· we d
o not know why the goddess Athena has chosen to so favo
r you above us all, but we shall remain grateful if you can r
eveal unto us the very secret to your sudden riches."

THEIR PLIGHT SADDEN THE RICH BASILEUS AND HE FELT D
EEPLY SORRY FOR HIS FRIENDS

"Hmmm, I feel your plights deeply my dear friends and it is

not my desire that you should not prosper; for when you p rosper, the city of Athens also prospers and the level of po verty and suffering is reduced. You seek for the secret to m y riches which of course I shall reveal to you··· i am sure yo u all know how I started life as a slave to many masters unt il I became a free man as you are. I had no privileges which young men do enjoy these days, and I had no special educ ation nor was I born into a rich home. I also have worked h ard and sorted after money but I never increased in wealth , the harder I worked the more frustrated I became and th e more money I chased after the more unaccountable I be came and my debts grew so rapidly."

ANTONIO: "Sorry my Lord, do you mean to say that hard w ork does not enrich a man?"

The truth about Riches

"I wish it did my friends, look at the craftsmen at the Agor a, the miners, the blacksmith, and the carpenters, do they not work hard?" Of course they do, "but has their hard wo rk made them rich?" No. "They work much harder than all of us seated here but gain so much little than us all, this sh ows that it is not hard work···let me ask you again, does th e son of a wealthy man need to work very hard to inherit h is portion of wealth? Of course not because it is his right, s omeone else has worked so hard to accumulate that wealt h for him, but this does not take the place of hard work. I l earnt that hard work only increases a man's chance of gett ing rich when such a man discovers the secret path to rich es and start walking in it···

When I found this truth for myself, I ceased to chase after money and seek for better ways to make money chase aft er me; I realized that it is not money that enriches a man b ut money only serves as an evidence of a man's riches, it is not everywhere you see money that you see riches, everyb ody deals with money every day; the laborers are paid thei r wages, the traders handle money every day, but does tha t mean they are rich? Of course not, it is not every where y ou see money that you see riches but you cannot see riche s without lots of money accompanying it, because money i s an evidence of riches but riches is not an evidence of mo ney. So, when a man set his heart after money, that does n ot mean he is after riches."

HMMM, GO ON BASILEUS, YOU SPEAK WELL, FOR GREAT T RUTH LIES WITHIN YOUR TOUNGUE AND WE NEVER THOU GHT IT SO

The Secret

"It is true, I myself never thought it so. And because I kne w it not, I labored so hard under the sun and chased so pas sionately after money but I only wasted both my hard wor k and money in vain. Then, I sought out to find out what w as the secret to riches and there it was all the while I never knew···

26

I discovered that the secret to riches was hidden in WISDO M!

WISDOM?!!! They asked in exclamation

YES MY FRIENDS, WISDOM. That was the secret that made me grew rich, I sort after a wise heart which led me to the path of riches. And about this path, I also noticed that a m an will only waste his effort, money, and time when he cha ses after riches with foolishness. For the fool and his mone y soon part ways. WISDOM directs the labor of a man and also his money and time, and until a man finds wisdom, he cannot prosper in his ways. He will remain blind to the pat h of riches. It is like a traveler who has no map to direct his course and embarks on a costly journey in the wrong direc tion; the faster he runs and the harder he works, the quick er he arrives at the wrong destination and the more frustr ated he becomes because he is not on the right course. His ignorance shall waste away his effort and until he embrace s wisdom, he cannot walk in the path of prosperity nor can he profit from his hard labor"

Anakletos: "Now I see, why my hard work never profited me or my money valuable to me, I never considered wisdo m as this important, for I thought in my heart that if a man could work very hard and chase after money, he shall beco me rich in due course. Well, Basileus, you have indeed spo ken wisely, but how do we get this wisdom you speak of th at can lead us into the path of prosperity just like it led you ?"

BASILEUS GAVE THEM A SMILE BEFORE SPEAKING OUT an

d he picked an owl (*the owl is a tetradrachm silver coin use d by Athenians as currency, and one owl contains four drac hma*) and asked them, "What is this in my hand?" "An owl coin" they replied "good and what can you see on the owl coin?" ANTONIO then replied, "On one side is the image o f the virgin goddess Athena, and on the other side is the im age of an owl-*the owl of Athena*" "Very true, Antonio, now what do both the virgin goddess Athena and the owl repre sents?" PATIOS replied, "They both represent wisdom, kn owledge and insight" "Very good Patios, you've spoken tr uthfully, on this coin you use every day to buy and sell is wi sdom inscribed on both sides. It tells you that you cannot h ave this piece of coin without wisdom. In fact, it is impossi ble to live a life of abundance without the wisdom needed to earn it. And those who lack this wisdom will end up wor shiping the money but those who gain the wisdom will lear n how to use the money to favor their paths.

We know very well what Sophocles does say about wisdo m in his plays, that, "Wisdom outweighs any wealth"

And such is the reality of riches that to rule over it or accu mulate it, a man must arm himself with wisdom and great wisdom in that"

AND THEY ALL BECAME VERY SHOCKED AT THE REVELATIO N OF BASILEUS, THAT THE SECRET THEY SOUGHT AFTER EA CH DAY AND NIGHT WAS IN THEIR HANDS ALL THEIR YEAR S OF LABOUR AND THEY NEVER LOOKED AT IT NOR THOUG HT THE COIN CARRIED THE GREATEST SECRET TO RICHES

In quest for Riches

Basileus then went on to say, "In my quest for wisdom, I d iscovered that Wisdom comes in five fold and a man shoul d possess all: the first been Discovery, the second-learning, the third-experience, the fourth-deeds and the last, rewar d. The first reveals to you, the second teaches you, the thir d shows you, the fourth requires your doing, and the last b lesses and pays you in profits. In my early days, I served un der different masters and learned different things in differ ent ways from all of them, some I learnt of their successes and others of their failures and in all these learning I grew wiser.

Once by the temple in the Acropolis, I was sent by my mas ter to bring a message to the Teacher and when I met him, I told him, "my master sent me a message to you" and he asked me, "Who are you?" I replied, "I am a slave unto my master" and he looked at me with great pity, and exhaled, then said to me, "you are a fine man Basileus although per ishing in bondage because of the misfortunes of life, but g o back home and think over it, for I see a free man bond in the slave you have now become" and I was shocked and m oved by his sayings, for no man had spoken to me in such a manner, these were the words that led me to discover mys elf and that night I saw a new part of me which was hidden and trapped down for years, the Teacher revealed to me my true self and from that day on, I began to sought ways of been a free man.

I began to detest the life of a slave each time I see how beautiful the life of a free man is, I paid more visit to the Teacher in secrets and he was willing to help set me free, he became my first light and exposed me to great knowledge and books. I then worked extra hard to gather the money I could and when I succeeded, I gave it to the Teacher who then approached my master and requested him to sell me off as a favor to the gods, for he needed more slaves in the temple. My master could not say no to the Teacher who happens to also be the Priest and out of respect for him, my master sold me to him and this was how I became a free man. The Teacher bought me and made me a free man.

My friends, I tell you, the first thing wisdom does is to set a man free.

You have said I dominate the market which is why your purses grow leaner but that is not true for one man's abundance is not a reason for another man's poverty. Since the day I discovered that there is more than enough for everyman, I worry little about another man's wealth and focused on building mine.

AND WITH THESE WORDS BASILEUS DISMISSED HIS NOBLE VISITORS WHO AGREED TO COME BACK ANOTHER DAY WITH OTHER MERCHANTS WHO MIGHT BE INTERESTED TO LISTEN TO THE WISDOM OF BASILEUS AND HOW HE ACCUMULATED HIS RICHES.

CHAPTER

3

DESIRES OF THE RICH

"Regard your name as the richest jewel you can possibly be possessed of – for credit is like fire; when once you have kindled it you may easily preserve it, but if you once extinguish it, you will find it an arduous task to rekindle it again. The way to gain a good reputation is to endeavor to be what you desire to appear."

Socrates

Become what you desire to appear.

SAID THE PHILOSOPHER TO HIS DISCIPLES; Socrates, Athens' most renowned and controversial philosopher who had gained great reputation and respect from the Athenians through his teachings and lifestyle had worked most of his life first as a mason following his father's craft to support his family before taking the life of a philosopher of which he hardly could support his family with. His teachings did not bring material wealth to him and died a poor man. His last words [*spoken to Crito his student*] after found guilty and sentenced to death by drinking of the Hemlock poison were of debt to his disciple, he said to him on his dead bed, *"Crito, we owe a cock to Asclepius. Do pay it. Don't forget"* *"Of course' said Crito "Do you want to say anything else?"* There was no reply to the question and he gave up the ghost. But after his death, Athens began to experience the wealth of Socrates teachings, although he was sentenced to death because the Athenians thought he was *"corrupting the youths"* and *"Refusing to recognize the gods recognized by the states"** but unknowingly to them, he was creating a new generation of freemen and great thinkers and also liberating Athenians from the enslavement of what they called gods, his desire was for all men to know that they were also themselves gods and they can do all that their minds could possibly conceive. His famous words were, "KNOW THYSELF"

Socrates, though poor in the physical but was rich in thoughts and his riches was transferred to many others who were able to teach others how to transfer such riches even from their minds to their purses.

...

ANTONIO and his friends decided to visit Rich Basileus once more that he might reveal to them the secret ways of riches and how they can also prosper in their trades. In their last visit, most of them could barely sleep for they had to ponder so hard on how foolish they had been with their hard works, time, and money. They all learnt that it is not hard work that enriches a man but WISDOM and that wisdom is what makes a man's hard work profitable.

Hard work profits more only when it is tied to a wealthy ideal; this they learnt from rich Basileus.

The suicide of Socrates, 339 BC," Eyewitness to History, www.eyewitnesstohistory.com (2003).

The feast

AT HIS HOME, the Young and Rich Basileus was feasting with his friends. So much was available for everyone: The best of wines, beef, different dishes from faraway lands, entertainers everywhere and the most influential men of Athens. The occasion was very colorful.

Antonio and his friends came when the feast was on. They met with one of the servants at the gate and enquired of him.

Anakletos: "Excuse us, please what is happening? Is your master celebrating a special occasion today?"

The Servant with a broad smile responded, "Yes Sir, today, Master is a year old and wishes to celebrate with family and friends"

Antonio: "Hmm, this is good to the ears, although we never knew but we must have arrived in a good time then, please can we see him?"

"Yes sir, although he is crowded but you can find your way to him"

AND THEY WENT THROUGH THE CROWD AND HAD ACCESS TO HIM

PATIOS: "How I so wish I were Basileus, I would have been living this kind of enviable life of luxury"

ANTONIO: "Not alone Patios, I also wish I had as much slaves and buyers as Basileus, I would have become a Lord amongst others"

ANAKLETOS: "Hmmm that is true, I had also always wished I had the brilliant connections and loyalty of friends as does Basileus, I would have been able to sell off lots of my good with great profits like he does"

THEY KEPT MAKING THEIR WISHES AS THEY SOUGHT AFTER RICH BASILEUS AND ALAS! THEY FOUND HIM

Basileus: "O! My dear friends, I see you have made it once more, and I must say I am very pleased to see you. Please feel free to enjoy whatever your heart desires, for today is a special day for me" he smiled cheerfully.

Antonio: "our dear friend Basileus, it is great we are here and we celebrate with you on this special day, although we came to seek more of your wisdom but were met with this occasion, so we wish to take our leave and return another day"

Basileus: "O no my friends, you have come a long way to see me, so I should attend to your needs. Tarry a little longer and enjoy the feast then we shall talk more tonight and when it is late, I have many rooms to host you all"

WITH THIS THEY WERE SO GLAD AND TARRIED A LITTLE LONGER WHILE THEY ENJOYED EVERY PART OF THE FEAST TILL THE END

....

Desires of the Rich

Basileus: "You are welcomed once more my friends and I hope you all enjoyed yourselves throughout the feast"

Anakletos: "Master Basileus, we had never experienced such a bountiful feast as this in Athens for so long, the food, the wine, the gifts, the entertainers, the personalities, the beauty, and the expense of the event. You must have lavished so much money into making this day a grand one"

Basileus: he laughed a little, "Thank you my friend Anakletos, I am much happy you all enjoyed yourselves. So, to what honor do I have your visit once more"

Antonio: "Yes our noble friend, you are indeed a rich and powerful man in Athens, and today only reveals how prosperous your life is and how much abundance you live in, we have come once more because of the words you spoke to us the last time, most of us could not sleep at night and only saw how wasteful we had been with our hard work, money, and time, so we decided to pay you one more visit to know more on how we can profit from our labor under the sun and prosper as you have prospered"

Patios: "it is true Rich Basileus, indeed we have wasted so much energy and profit just to make a little to feed our families and provide the basic needs of life but we lack the abundance to make life good. Today, my eyes have been opened to what riches could do in a man's life. At the feast, I saw the expensive silk given out as gifts, the jewelries, and shoes; I ate tonight dishes from the Persians and Egyptians, I saw how happy the orphans were as they ate from your table, your servants are like free men and bless the gods for having you as a master; the emperor was here, and also prominent senators, and philosophers, the priest was also around. You have indeed make wealth of both people and substance. How can we become like you, Rich Basileus?"

Basileus: "Well, you have spoken much and flattered me but I myself am a common man like you and of little words, but I shall tell you the best I can how I achieved all I possess and what worked for me and helped me to become what I am today, for I see a sincere heart in you all. Now, do you remember what the Philosopher always ends his teachings with? He does say, *"Become what you desire to appear"*. Many know not the truth behind those words but those were the words I started with. I asked myself this question, *'Young Basileus, what do you desire to appear like in a decade?'* and I saw many things and desired so many things but as the Greek Philosopher Epicurus will say, *'If thou wilt make a man happy, add not unto his riches but take away from his desires'* I discovered that my many desires had made me sober and unfulfilled, so I began to cut down my desires in order to strengthen my utmost desire. I did not desire the gold, the silk, the food, or the spices. I desired the two things every rich man desires and these were – HAPPINESS and FULFILLMENT.

Things the Rich go after

I saw that the rich seek more to be happy and fulfilled than any other thing else, so they did many things to gain happiness and fulfillment. They build houses, make a lot of money, wear the best of cloths, build temples, marry beautiful wives, have sound children, travel to different parts of the world, give to the society, gain positions and names, live in abundance, and buy whatever their hearts desires. I saw that riches although not happiness in itself was able to reduce the worries of a man and afford almost all the things that could make him fulfilled. Then, when I gained wisdom, I set my heart to increase my earnings. To build wealth and also maintain it".

Antonio: "but Basileus, does that mean desire alone cannot enrich man?"

Basileus: "Well, I wish it could, desire alone cannot enrich a man but it can excite the passion and fuel the effort of a man. If a man desires an unleavened bread, his attention will be focused on getting just the bread but if a man desires to build a bread house and supply an entire village, his attention will not be on getting an unleavened bread to eat and live but to build a bread house, and employ a lot of workers who can produce a lot of bread for sale and he will not only have bread to eat but also make huge returns by selling of bread. Your desire directs your attention.

What you desire you begin to see everywhere. When you desire a beautiful damsel, you begin to see damsels around, when you desire a ship you begin to see all kinds of ships, and when you desire riches you begin to see riches in everything. That is the key, your desire changes your focus.

You see, the philosopher is wise but not rich and you may ask yourself why? This is because his desire is after wisdom and not after riches. If he desires riches, his attention will be shifted and he will begin to use his wisdom to accumulate wealth but the teachings of wealth are different from the teachings of philosophy. He must begin to learn the teachings of wealth, he must be financially conscious, and become wise in handling finances otherwise his wealth will profit him not."

HMM, THIS SOUNDS TRUE BASILEUS

WELL MY FRIENDS, today you can see for yourselves what riches can turn an ordinary event into. I would have chosen not to celebrate and wished myself a happy life and live on just like the average man will do, but I say, No, let me make others merry with me and make the day glorious and unlike other men who would borrow money to celebrate or use their hard earned money to impress others, I am not of the two kinds, for I spend not out of lack but out of abundance, I spend the excess of my profit and not my income. What I used for this celebration was out of the excess my wealth had accumulated for me, so I would not have to worry how to repay back myself because at this point in my life, the more I spend the more I gain. And today, this feast has not only made me happy but has made a lot of people happy and has also fed the one who has nothing to eat at home for the night.

You yourselves have testified of what riches can do and it made you began to desire it because your hearts are now set on it and how to grow rich like myself; when some came in, they saw only the food because their desire at that moment was to eat and get satisfied, others saw connections because they desired to meet with prominent political figures, but yours was riches because you desired to be rich. You saw the riches in everything and not just the food, the people, and the gifts. So I tell you my friends, you must cut down all unnecessary desires and passion in order to strengthen your greatest desire at this moment which is to become rich, happy, free, and fulfilled. THIS IS THE SECOND STEP AFTER HAVING WISDOM.

AND THAT NIGHT THEY WENT TO BED WITH THEIR DESIRES MORE HIGHTENED THAN EVER BEFORE, EACH ONE THINKING AND MEDITATING ON THE BENEFITS OF A RICH LIFE.

CHAPTER

4

IN PURSUIT OF RICHES
Not life, but a good life is to be chiefly valued

Socrates

Themorning before the merchants left the house of Basileus; they were served with delicate breakfast and ate with Basileus at his table

ANTONIO: "O! Good Basileus, you are indeed a very generous man and the gods have prospered you this much, we appreciate every bit of your advice and the gifts from your table. Last night, I slept with only the desire to become very rich and someday invite you also for a dinner in my place"

AND THEY ALL LAUGHED

BASILEUS: "Am happy to have you my friends and will someday also love to dine with you at your tables, but for now you should spare the time to make good use of my table...AND THEY LAUGHED MORE...Before you leave this morning, I have a story to tell you on the pursuit of riches and also a code of merchants to hand over to you"

THAT IS GREAT MY LORD SAID PATIOS, WE'LL APPRECIATE IT, FOR EVERY WORD THAT COMES FROM YOUR MOUTH BRINGS FORTH WISDOM AND LIBERATION

Well my friends, This Persian story has been passed down from generation to generation by wise men and teachers to their disciples and to men who seek great riches because of its deep morals on wealth for which every man who desires gold should know and I shall also share it with you this day:

Acres of Diamonds

The story was of a wealthy Persian man named Al Hafed who lived not far from the river Indus. Al Hafed owned a very large farm with orchards, grain fields and gardens. He was a contented and wealthy man - contented because he was wealthy and wealthy because he was contented. One day there visited this old farmer one of those ancient Buddhist priest and he sat down by Al Hafed's fire and told him how this world of ours was created.

After that, the priest told Al Hafed about diamonds. He said to him, "If you had a handful of diamonds you could purchase a whole country for yourself and with a mine of diamonds you could place your children upon thrones through the influence of their great wealth."

Desire for Diamonds

Al Hafed heard all about diamonds and how much they were worth, and went to his bed that night a poor man – not that he had lost anything, but poor because he was discontented and discontented because he thought he was poor. He said: "I want a mine of diamonds!" so he lay awake all night, and early in the morning sought out the priest.

He awoke the priest out of his dreams and said to him, "Will you tell me where I can find diamonds?" The priest said, "Diamonds? What do you want with diamonds?" "I want to be immensely rich" said Al Hafed, "but I don't know where to go." "Well," said the priest, "if you will find a river that runs over white sand between high mountains, in those sands you will always see diamonds." "Do you really believe that there is such a river?" "Plenty of them, plenty of them; all you have to do is just go and find them, then you have them." Al Hafed said, "I will go." So he sold his farm, collected his money at interest, left his family in charge of a neighbor, and away he went in search of diamonds.

The quest

He began very well, to the mines, at the Mountains of Moon. Afterwards he went around countries of the world, and at last, when his money was all spent, and he was in rags, wretchedness and poverty, he stood on the shore of the sea feeling so dejected and when a tidal wave came rolling through the Pillars of Hercules, the poor, dejected, and awful Al Hafed could not resist the temptation to cast himself into the tidal wave, and so was it that he sank beneath its foaming crest, never to rise in this life again. So his dream of diamonds ended in the sea.

Now Al Hafed's successor, the new farm owner, led his camel out into the garden to drink, and as that camel put its nose down into the clear water of the garden brook, Al Hafed's successor noticed a curious flash of light that reflected all the colors of the rainbow, and he took that curious pebble to his house and left it on the mantel to serve as a door post support, then went on his way and forgot all about it.

A few days after that, this same old priest who told Al Hafed how diamonds were made, came in to visit his successor, when he saw that sparkling flash of light at the mantel. He rushed up and said, "Here is a diamond – here is a diamond! Has Al Hafed returned?" "No, no; Al Hafed has not returned and that is not a diamond; that is nothing but a stone; we found it right out here in our garden." "But I know a diamond when I see it," said the priest, "that is a diamond!"

Hidden treasures

Then together they rushed to the garden and stirred up the white sands with their fingers and found others more beautiful, more valuable diamonds than the first. The whole farm was acres of diamonds buried in them but Al Hafed knew not. Had Al Hafed remained at home and dug in his own cellar or his own garden, instead of suffering dejection, starvation, poverty and death in a strange land, he would have had "acres of diamonds" – for every acre, yes, every shovelful of that old farm afterwards revealed the gems which since have decorated the crowns of monarchs

And this we know was the story behind the diamond mines of Golconda, the most magnificent diamond mines in all history of mankind.

...

So my friends, there may be one of you seated here as Al Hafed. Who knows not that true riches lies within him. For truly, the very rich are first rich in mind and then in possession, and it is the richness within them that attracts the riches outside of them.

In the acquisition of wealth, the mind of a man is most important and must be made wealthy in order not to rust in poverty. My desire today is for you all to be free and to first look within yourselves for the hidden treasures buried in you before taken over by the desires to get immensely rich like Al Hafed. And on this day I stand more to you as the priest who told Al Hafed about diamonds which inspired him, tonight I will also tell you about riches and inspire you but do not act like Al Hafed and forsake the riches around you for the riches you know not.

Every gift is valuable

The weary man should know that most surprisingly, riches often comes dressed in rags you hardly can recognize and also from unthinkable places you can ever imagine, so no man should despise anything nor any opportunity at hand.

A man who is always funny with others may not realize that been funny and making others laugh could be the hidden diamond which could earn him a royal place in the King's court as the King's jester and thereby setting him free from all lacks and bitterness of life, neither knows not a beautiful damsel who despises character, integrity and chastity, that by adding these virtues to her beauty she could become the envy of both men and gods and hence put herself in the empire of great abundance and wealth of kings and noble men. You may be gifted in trade, music, writing, painting, politics, philosophy or a nice craft; these are what riches look for when it passes by, it notices the works of your hands and finds a way to prosper them. An idle hand drives away riches and a lazy heart shuts the door to any possibility. And just like the great teacher Socrates will say, "LET HIM THAT WOULD MOVE THE WORLD FIRST MOVE HIMSELF"

AND THEY WERE ALL MOVED BY THE WORDS OF BASILEUS, FOR IT WAS ENRICHING AND REFRESHING, AND AS THEY PLANED TO LEAVE, RICH BASILEUS WENT TO HIS INNER ROOM AND BROUGHT OUT A SCROLL OUT OF A HIDDEN BOX AND HANDED IT TO THEM

Basileus: "Here is the Code I promised you, I only have this copy with me so you must handle it with much care for I value it greatly. I was handed this code to study and be familiar with them for they were codes written down to guide a merchant in his every trade and quest, so have this and make good use of it"

HE HANDED THE SCROLL TO THEM WITH A SMILE AND THEY COLLECTED IT WITH GREAT JOY AND THANKED HIM FOR HIS GESTURES

"...And before you leave, do not forget Aesop's feeble about the man and the wooden god, it relates well to what we have been saying" AND HE WALKED THEM OUT

The Man and the Wooden God

IN the old days men used to worship stocks and stones and idols, and prayed to them to give them luck. It happened that a Man had often prayed to a wooden idol he had received from his father, but his luck never seemed to change. He prayed and he prayed, but still he remained as unlucky as ever. One day in the greatest rage he went to the Wooden God, and with one blow swept it down from its pedestal. The idol broke in two, and what did he see? An immense number of coins flying all over the place

*Acres of diamonds by Russell Conwell

Chapter

5

THE CODE OF MERCHANTS

D ue to the need to succeed in their trade, some of the ancient Athenian merchants whom have mastered the art of trade took their time to establish a code which will help guide the new merchants and even old ones who lack the skill to establish a successful trade. They discovered that almost all of them who prospered in their trade had one time or the other used the various codes to prosper, so they agreed to write it down and pass it on to merchants who wish to prosper as well.

But as time went on, the code became scarce and was soon misplaced. Copies of the code were hard to come by and the few ones available were now hidden and used secretly as a weapon to dominate the majority of merchants who were ignorant of the code and could not have access to it. The code turned out to become a great secret to be treasured by great merchants and Basileus was amongst the most fortunate to have been handed a copy of the code by the priest himself so he could study, learn, and apply it. From the foundations of his business to the very top, Basileus had used the code in every of his dealings to build a great business empire.

Today, he decided to avail the same codes to his treasured friends who also seek to prosper in their trades.

There were twelve laws buried within the code:

THE CODE OF MERCHANTS

1) The customer is King

Your customer is the reason why you are in business. Never ignore or treat unkindly a buyer because you have others, that one buyer is as valuable as the hundred buyers you boast of. He should be treated as a King and be given all the necessary attention he deserves, never allow him leave your stand the same, and do not only sell the goods to him which he will take away and leave, sell also to him your attitude, affection, and kindness which he will keep bringing back in exchange for more goods. A smile from you will cover a multitude of lost.

2) Quality exceeds Quantity

Never sacrifice the need for more over the need of value. Better a piece of diamond than hundreds of brass and better a pure gold than a bucket full of clay. Quality must always exceed quantity. Never lower the standard because of patronage and soon you will be crowded. As corrupt as a man's heart is, he still seeks for quality and the best of things; no one wants a fake although many will try to sell a fake. Men still pursue excellence, so do not be accustomed to the cheep things of life, always go for value and quality, this pays more in the later.

3) Pay yourself

As you pay others pay also yourself. Every merchant deserves his pay. You have not only employed people to work for you but have also employed yourself to work for you. You should pay yourself a fix amount to be free from the temptations of consuming your profits thinking you own all in the business and can freely spend the way you like. Pay yourself and do not go beyond the expense of your pay and for every penny you spend outside your pay, you must refund it. Your profit is your seed for the expansion of your trade, do not burn it up carelessly.

4) Earn as you learn

Learning without earning is futile. For every knowledge or skill gained, there must be an equivalent income drawn to it. We learn not only to know but also to prosper. Whatever will not benefit you is not worth so much of your attention, devote your time, attention and energy into knowing and learning things that will enlarge, enrich, and enthrone you in life.

5) Let your greed not exceed your interest

Greed seems inevitable in business but never allow your greed to exceed your interest. Learn to make the cut and know when to walk away. Greed is like a sweet honey dropping from a bee wasp; you get carried away by the sweetness and forget the deadly sting at the top end. It is same greed that makes the fly follow the corps into the grave. Be happy with your profit, where you can get more get it but do not get it at the expense of others – that is greed. There is nothing bad in striving for more, it is bad and becomes greed when you strive at the expense of others, and you put them in suffering and impoverishment to enrich yourself. This is greed and it will get back at you on a good day. Put a knife to your throat.

6) Inspire your Buyers

There is a need for the extraordinary. People are naturally moved by something spectacular, thrilling, exciting, and extreme, it over rides their thinking and consume their desires. People want to be inspired at all cost; they want to see something new and creative. Your duty is not only to impress them; your duty is also to inspire them, to amaze them and to blow their minds. At this point you must add great flavor, uniqueness, and spark to your work or product, some ingenuity that will glue their attention completely to your work without them realizing the presence of your competitors.

7) Learn languages

You will earn more if you can communicate more. You must command as many languages as you possibly can, wherever you find yourself, learn their language and lifestyle. Be like them for your business sake. Do not just learn the spoken languages also learn the unspoken ones; people speak more when they are not talking. Their eyes speaks, so do their hands, ears, legs, spirits, minds, and all that they are; your duty is to observe them, learn from them, speak like them, and know the best moments to make your sale. This virtue alone will make you more acceptable anywhere; people get impressed seeing a total stranger trying to accept their way of life.

8) Pay your workers well

A stingy merchant will soon be ruined by his stewards. People cannot starve and work efficiently for you; they will soon find other means to survive by stealing from you. Treat your workers well and they will protect your interest, they will labor more for you smiling. Let the motivation be stronger than the pain and they will endure almost anything.

9) Expand

Do not remain fixed in one place, after establishing a trade in a city, begin to expand it. Open up new branches in different regions, put in faithful stewards to manage it for you, move to other cit and do the same. By this, you are growing like the human body from a cell into a tissue then an organ and finally a system. As you expand in branches also expand in skills and potentials. Expose your loyalist to acquiring new and better skill to manage and better expand the trade. Never limit yourself in a fix trade.

10) Conceal your strengths

It is better for them to see you weak and later discover you are strong than to see you strong and later discover you are weak. Your originality lies in your strength, and it is yours to keep. The secret of every unique product is its strength and what gives it an edge over its competitors. Conceal your strengths, clean the traces, and polish the scared faces of your work. There are things only the merchant can know about his trade and no one else, when you find such thing, bury it within and focus on the superficial look.

11) Never promise what you cannot keep

Integrity is the soul of a business. Do not hasten to impress your customer with empty promises, you may get away with it but will lose a faithful buyer. Let your word be your bond. Do not tell a customer to come tomorrow when you know you will fail him, the customer is you greatest tool of advert, when he is fulfilled, he goes home impressed and tell his friends and family about you, he recommends you to others and direct them to always patronize you because you are trustworthy. Never promise what you cannot keep.

12) Mind your family and friends

A good merchant is not the one who makes the greatest of profit alone but the one who makes the best of profits and still have time for his love, family, and friends. He avails himself to them and also helps them at the points of need. Do not allow the desire of riches possess your love for family and friends. What will be the use of all your income if no one can benefit from it? Make time for your family: your wife, your children, your parents, your siblings, your relatives, and your friends.

CHAPTER

6

THE FOOL'S GOLD

"By right means, if you can, but by any means, make money"

Horace

O N ANOTHER DAY

With his white beard and dressed in an expensive purple cloak, rich Basileus was seated on a well knitted mat with his friends in the free space within the house. There were servants going up and down attending to issues and some serving them with wine and fruits... and he began speaking with them

BASILEUS: "So again my friends, I say unto you, desire to be rich in this world also; for it is better to be rich than to be poor. But in riches do not be fooled that it is happiness, for a man must find something greater than riches which lies in love to be happy. Strive not to be poor either, for there is neither happiness nor wellbeing in it and the poor have no power or say in this world ruled by the rich and powerful.

A man may give himself an excuse saying, "Riches do not bring happiness", but I ask such a man, "Does poverty then bring happiness?"

Do not be fooled by following the lot of those who have failed or have given up on their dreams and hopes and now seek for an excuse not to be wealthy, for even the Creator himself is not poor and did not create men to be poor or made riches to be evil. Although the poor will always remain with us but there are no people on earth marked poor for even if they were born poor, there is always a chance for them to decide to be rich. Take a look at the beauty and abundance of the universe and you will know that we were created to lead a life of abundance, love, and happiness.

With riches comes influence and many friends, favor chases after the rich more easily than the poor and such men become easily admired and envied by many. The life of the rich my friends, is full of merriment and great pleasures; yet, a man must have a reason to be rich, and not be carried away by the pleasures it offers otherwise, he shall corrupt himself and misery will befall him.

And also, be careful, for many in an attempt to get rich have been fooled for they desire it too quickly and by so doing, tried to keep their backs from the heat of the sun without knowing that riches has wings and flies away from the lazy hands, and the sluggish heart. The very life of idleness and sleep drives it away quickly.

AND PATIOS INTERRUPTED

PATIOS: "Sorry rich master, what do you mean by been fooled for their desires to get rich quickly? For every man desires quick riches, so why speak against such?"

BASILEUS: "Yes Patios, I do not stop a man from desiring to become rich quickly, but that he should be careful, for many men have lost their possessions in an attempt to attain quick riches. When I traveled to Milos, I learnt of the story of a young man, who desired quick riches; he was young, very zealous, and full of energy.

And Like other young men of his age thriving in Rome, Claudius also desired immense gold. So many were his wishes and so many were his wants. But one problem with the young man – he desires riches too quickly, and this deprived him of focus.

The Dreamer

Today Claudius wants to be a physician because he sees how beautiful the town's Physician attends to his patients and how much he makes and Tomorrow Claudius then aspires to be a Soldier because he sees how the King spoils the Soldiers with bounties after a victorious battle. And the next time you see Claudius, he will tell you he wants to be a Law giver...

At this point, the three men began laughing... then he continued

Claudius dreamt of becoming so many things that he couldn't stay focused on one thing. If he starts a trade and gets bored, he quits it for another, his mind toasted to and fro like the whirl wind, and his heart was burned with too many passions and goals that every day leaves him the same or more miserable. Many nights met Claudius dreaming of riches and most time wakes up frustrated to find himself in his poor little hut, he did wished his dreams were real and often goes back to sleep again in order to dream one more time maybe the gods will deliver a magic portion for riches unto him.

Friends of a feather flock together

Now Claudius had a friend called Gaius, he was no different from Claudius himself, for both were dreamers. And on many nights, they both will sit under the fig tree discussing about their dreams and hopes and how rich they wanted to become in life, then after their talks, they will wave at each other goodbye and go to sleep.

On one of those nights, a conversation broke and Gaius told Claudius about the new Alchemist who came to town and his willingness to teach a select few how to transform ordinary metals into gold.

Claudius responded:

Waw! That is great! How possible?!!!

Gaius: "I do not know but I think he possesses some hidden powers that could transform ordinary metals into gold."

That night was like a dream come through for Claudius, for he was so happy and they both agreed to see the Alchemist as soon as possible, who knows, this might be the breakthrough opportunity they had been waiting for.

...

Now, it was the age of Alchemy where scientist, philosophers and other desperate people who desired riches ventured into it to make gold. Many spend their last penny acquiring the skill and in few days become wealthy by the act. Although Alchemy was a rare thing in Rome and was even prohibited, but desperate men went as far as the secret hole could lead to get rich. And the new Alchemist in town came in secret and only a select few knew about him and were ready to patronize him.

...

Alchemist: "You said you desire gold?"

Claudius: "Yes we do and it is for this course we sought after thee"

Alchemist: "Then it is a good course you have chosen, for many have not yet found this secret path to riches, they work so hard under the heat of the day with nothing to show forth. But the gods have listened to the cry of a few lucky ones amongst us and have granted us a much easier way to accumulate wealth. I shall show to you all that you need to know about Alchemy but you must promise not to circulate this secret knowledge to the common man on the street and also, the knowledge you desire for will cost you a little, I hope you know that?"

Gaius: "Yes we do our lord; ask of us the cost and we shall provide"

Alchemist: "Very well then, for I see you are much prepared... it shall cost you each 20 pieces of gold coins out of which I shall teach you the how and give you the ingredients you need to make your own gold coin"

And noticing a bit of doubt in them, he went on to say...

"You must know that money beget money and what I have for you and what I ask of you are incomparable, for I desire to assist you seeing you are young men and have risked your lives sorting after me at this dead hour of the night. So much wealth I say awaits any man who possesses this skill, for he shall have the liberty to create his own wealth"

...

He went inside and brought out some portions and three ordinary coins. He then sat in front of them and began mixing the portions and after everything, he placed the three ordinary metal coins into the mixture and washed them properly and behold gold coins were made right in front of them.

At the sight of this, the men became inspired seeing how easy and real it is to make gold out of ordinary metals. Their desire for gold grew even stronger.

...

After the meeting, both Claudius and Gaius were not very excited, for 20 pieces of gold coin was huge money and could get them a pretty nice home. But after many thoughts and talking over the benefits of making as many gold coins they want in a day, they decided that the skill was worth the cost and will go any length to acquire it.

Claudius: "After we learn this, we could make as much gold coin in secret as we can, and we can also charge others who want to learn it from us"

Gaius: "I agree with you my friend, and I think we should get all the gold we can borrow to acquire this secret knowledge to riches"

Then, they went about borrowing money by making promises to refund it as soon as possible and before the week runs out, they were able to gather 40 gold coins and went straight to the Alchemist. And on that night after paying the Alchemist, he then began showing them how to go about it.

The Alchemist took enough time and thought them how to do it but gave them a condition that the chemicals used must first be kept for 3 days before the start of work so that the elements in it can be strongly be active. He also repeated what he did by turning 3 more ordinary coins in front of them into gold coins and they were satisfied

Then he instructed them to be careful with the portions for they were rare and expensive to get. He gave them all they needed. So they left that night in rich spirits and with great excitement, for their labor will soon pay off.

...

Gaius: "Claudius! I think our dreams of riches is right before us, I never knew it was this easy to make riches"

Claudius: "so true my friend, I saw all that he did and they were real and so easy, and I learnt many people do not know of this."

...

Now after 3 days, Claudius and Gaius got as many ordinary metal coins as they could and where ready and very excited to start making as much gold as they desired. They then began by mixing the portions appropriately and then putting in the metal coins and stirring. They stirred and stirred looking out desperately for the gold coins but unfortunately, nothing showed up. They went over again and stirred, still the magic coin did not show up. This they kept repeating all through the night in deep sweat but to no avail.

...

Claudius: "What is wrong Gaius? why are the coins not turning into gold?"

Gaius: "I do not know myself and am surprised, or we missed a step?"

Claudius: "missed? No I do not think so, for we repeated it as many times as possible and nothing is working."

...

Then they gave it more try but nothing happened and in great disappointment and anguish, they gave up trying and agreed to see the Alchemist on the morrow. That night, there was no sleep for both of them as they waited desperately for the dawn in utter dejection.

At first sunlight, they arrived at the Alchemist house, and asked after him; behold he was lost. They asked the neighbors around but no one could relate to what the young men were saying, for all claimed not to know of any Alchemist. Tears of pain, anguish, disappointment, and regrets began dropping down their cheeks. And as they wallow in regrets, five other people came asking after same Alchemist with same complains as Claudius and Gaius. It was at this point that they realized they had been fooled and conned.

...

What they do not know was that the Alchemist was no Alchemist at all but a con master in the art. He had used people's desire to get rich quickly to fool them and get rich by their gold. This con master travels to different towns with same trick and never returns. When he gets to a town, he makes an arrangement with a dweller who goes out in secret telling people about an Alchemist in town who can teach them how to make gold of ordinary metals, and when the con master is done with his game, he rewards his partner and leave the city for good.

...

When Basileus finished the story, he beckoned on a servant for a cup of water to clear his throat as his friends thought deeply about the story he just finished saying.

BASILEUS: "So my friends, I know some of you might have fallen into the hands of men like the Alchemist and if you are not very careful, you may still fall into the hands of such men for the sake of quick riches. Do not be deceived, it is better to earn riches than stumble on one, for if a man earn his riches and then lost it, he can easily make it back but if he stumbles on it or is given it and loses it, it would be almost impossible to accumulate such riches back.

See the gambler who works hard in the day to put his whole money in one night for a lucky fortune, and the lazy man who awaits anxiously for his father's death or even hasten it that he may inherit his own portion of the inheritance and also a damsel who seeks not virtue but stay late in dark corners of the night to gain wealthy suitors for herself. They all end up in vanity and misfortune. It is more honorable my friends, to earn wealth than to stumble on it with ignorance.

AND WITH THESE WORDS, BASILEUS ENDED THE BREAK FAST WITH HIS GUEST AND GAVE THEM A SCROLL TO READ WHEN THEY GET BACK HOME WHICH WAS ONCE GIVEN TO HIM BY HIS TEACHER AT THE TEMPLE WHEN HE STRUGGLED TO BE A FREE MAN.

BASILEUS: "This scroll my friends you must find the time to read it and when we meet again I shall ask of your learning from it and to see what profit it has made to your desires for riches"

AND WITH THESE WORDS, HE DISMISSED THEM AND SAID HE WILL BE VERY BUSY SO THEY WOULD NOT GET TO MEET UNTIL AFTER THE FESTIVAL OF DIONYSUS.

CHAPTER

7

MASTER YOUR SKILLS

"Fortune cannot aid those who do nothing"

Sophocles

It's the month of Elaphebolion when visitors from far and near Athens come to celebrate the famous festival of Dionysia in honor of the Greek god Dionysius, the festival was introduced by the tyrant Pisistratus. BASILEUS again ran into his friends for they also made it to the memorable festival which had its peak at the performances in the theater of Dionysius where competitions of tragic plays were performed and winners awarded. The festival begins with marching of the statue of the god Dionysius (most times called the god of wine and the madness that follows drinking) from the temple to the theatre close to the Acropolis (the place for Athenian worship), the festival was full of wine and entertainment mainly dramas of both humor and tragedy. And it was in this very theatre just after the victory of the Athenians over the Persians at Salamis that great playwrights and inventors of dramas like Aeschylus, Euripides, and Sophocles made their names and impacts. Today is another day where younger playwrights and dramatist are to compete and exhibit both their tragic and humorous plays in the form of a trilogy.

Ever since the victory at salamis, the new Athenian ruler Pericles had spent so much time and money to encourage art, philosophy, architecture, and invention in Athens. He had embarked on the Massive construction of the Acropolis in order to return the Athenian's lost glory.

...

Basileus was accompanied by his three friends; Antonio, Anakletos, and Patios. They were all in high spirit as they sat to watch the tragic plays before them and enjoy the period.

BASILEUS: "I see you made it to the feast, it seems fickle fate has a lot to offer us."

With great smile and pleasure to meet Basileus again, Antonio responded, "very true Basileus, it is good to be in your company once more"

AND THEY ALL FOUND A PLACE AND SAT DOWN

BASILEUS: "so have you had time to go through the scroll I gave you?"

ANAKLETOS: "Not really but after the festival we shall find the time to go through it before we meet with you again"

Oedipus the King

BASILEUS: "It is good then, today's occasion is special and reminds me of the times of the great Sophocles and his tragic plays especially *Oedipus the King* which although won the second place but seems to be one of my favorite tragic stories"

ANAKLETOS: "True Basileus, although one was not privileged to see the play, but I learnt that Oedipus at the end fulfilled the prophecy of the Oracle who said he will shade the blood of his father and sleep with his mother"

BASILEUS: "Yes he did, the play was about King Laius and his wife Jocasta who after being told the prophecy that the child they had bore will kill his father and sleep with his mother decided to kill the child to prevent the prophecy from come true. The King ordered the Queen to kill the child and the Queen gave the child to her servant to kill by placing him at the mountain top, but the child was saved by a shepherd who took him to Corinth where King Polybus and his Queen Merope took in Oedipus as if he were their own child and brought him up. When Oedipus became a man and learnt he was not the true child of Polybus and Merope, he questioned them but they denied so he believed them but went further to ask the Delphic Oracle of who he truly was but the Oracle only told him the prophecy that befalls his life; that he will kill his father and sleep with his mother."

Patios: "Hmm that must be an unfortunate fate, so what did Oedipus then do to avoid such tragedy?"

BASILEUS: "He fled from Corinth thinking since King Polybus and Queen Merope were his parents, he would not harm them when he is far away, but that was his greatest mistake, for when he was on the run, he arrived at a crossroad where he met men from Thebes led by Laius his true father which he did not know and they argued whose right was it to cross the road, and when Laius was about to strike, Oedipus attacked and killed him and all the men with him leaving just one witness, and this fulfills part of the prophecy that he will kill his father"

ANTONIO: "That is really tragic, so how about sleeping with his mother?"

BASILEUS: "Yes, about his mother, he also fulfilled that. When Oedipus arrived Thebes he was able to solve the riddle of the Sphinx which said, *"What is the creature that walks on four legs in the morning, two at noon, and three in the evening?"* and Oedipus replied "Man" for man crawls on his four limbs as infant, walks on his two legs as adult, and uses the stick when old. This was how he won the riddle which had enslaved the city for long and the reward was that he be their king and have the hand of the Queen Jocasta (his true mother) as his wife, and so was it that he fulfilled the second prophecy that he would sleep with his mother.

PATIOS: "It is a brilliant tragedy and what happened to Oedipus when he discovered he had fulfilled the long prophecy he had been running away from all his life?"

BASILEUS: "He went mad, and was determined to kill his mother but she had already killed herself when she discovered the truth and Oedipus pierced his eyes and went blind and demanded he be exiled from the city. This was the end of Oedipus the King and a most tragic story for a man to have killed his own father and slept with his own mother"

AND AT THE END OF THE FESTIVAL AND DRAMAS, BASILEUS SPENT A LITTLE MORE TIME WITH HIS FRIENDS WHO ARE NOW BECOMING HIS DISCIPLES AS THEY TALKED ABOUT THE TRAGIC PLAY THEY JUST WATCHED.

ANTONIO: "I think today's play is a good one because it shows how great a man could be if he could only master his skill. The playwright was brilliant of his tragic play"

PATIOS: "I agree with you Antonio, the playwright was great and he had mastered every line of his play with the characters and was able to bring out the emotion from every bit of it or what do you say Master Basileus"

Exercising talents

BASILEU: "Very true, the play was great and that took a lot of mastery to produce such a powerful play, I met with the playwright at the end of the event and had a talk with him and he opened up to tell me that it took him and the team over a period of three months of consistent writing and practicing to perfect such a short and powerful play that lasted not more than an hour"

ANAKLETOS: "Three months?!"

BASILEUS: "Very well, three months of consistent rehearsal to produce such a spectacular play and I believe it was worth it, for a man must master his skill if he wishes to succeed with it. During the times of Sophocles, he would spend hours with other great playwright like Aeschylus to master the inventory of play, and after so many hours of meditation and practice, Sophocles was able to win the heart of Athenians through his plays, in fact, his plays enriched him and enthroned him into great positions. He became the commander of the army under

Pericles reign and also served as the priest of Amynos and also as a priest unto Asclepius the god of health, he carried out these sacred duties in his house before a temple was built unto Asclepius and prospered during his time so much that he was revered. His skills earned him a place in Athens and not because he was from a wealthy family but transformed the Athenian play"

ANTONIO: "Now you talk of mastering a skill, how much time than should a man devote to mastering a skill?"

BASILEUS: "Men vary in learning when it comes to mastering skill but if you observe most craftsmen in Athens and men of noble callings like the city physicians and law givers you will notice that they spend so many years in order to master their skill, some spend over seven years and others a little more to be masters of their skill. A young man who desires to be a merchant follows his master for over eight years to master the trade and around the age of 16 when male boys are equipped into the army, they spend over 25 years training to master the act of self defense. Let me ask you, have you not heard of Milo of cronus?"

ANAKLETOS: "Well, we have heard rumors and myth about his strength and deeds"

BASILEUS: "And what have you heard of both his strength and deeds?"

ANAKLETOS: "That he was a great fighter during his time and an undefeated champion in the wrestling of the

Olympic Games dedicated to Zeus the god of gods, and there was nothing that could match his strength"

PATIOS: "Yes, I also heard that he was able to save the life of the Philosopher Pythagoras by holding the pillar of a collapsing building all by himself so that the building will not crush the philosopher and he also escaped at the end"

ANTONIO: "I myself also learnt that he ones challenged the strongest of men and they could not bend his little finger nor were they able to open his hand to remove the fruit he held, and when he finally opened his hand, the fruit was uncrushed and untendered"

BASILEUS: "That is interesting, for I see you've actually heard a lot about him, I also learnt that men who participated in the act of fighting like Milo were separated from the ordinary people and trained with all severity to master their skill, they were denied of common pleasures like alcohol, sex, and unnecessary sleep. Day and night they were exposed to the heat of the sun and the cold of the night and at the end of their training, they would have become like the divine gods when they appear oiled and naked for the people of Athens to behold. I also heard of such stories that Milo trained himself by carrying of a bull right from it small to when it was fully grown and that made it easier for him to carry a full grown bull at one of the Olympics and later killed it with his bare hands and consumed it. Milo also was able to lead his fellow armies to fight against the Sybaris who were three times their number and they won the battle.

MASTER YOUR TRADE

Now I tell you the truth, so many are like Milo who become divine by virtue of training and mastering their skills and so ought to be a merchant. You should be good at a trade and master it until you can command it, for many trade men start a trade and when discouragement comes, they switch to another trade and so they keep switching and never grow in any. A good merchant defines his trade and make a name in it, he dwells upon that trade and grows gradually in it. He devotes his time to master every risk, loss, and profit making ways in his trade that he may prosper in it.

When you plant a seed today in a soil, and tomorrow you feel the soil is not good and you change it to another soil and the next day you change it and keep changing it, do you think the plant will thrive and grow? No it will perish for it was not given the time to grow its root deep down the soil to seek for nutrients in the earth and draw nourishment from it. When you find a good soil or trade, plant your seed or idea and money in it and begin to nurture it so it can grow, your attention should not be deviated, but stay focus and make it grow.

When I call the name Sophocles, you see a playwright; when I say Milo, you see a write; when I say Socrates, you see a Philosopher; and when I say Basileus, you see a merchant. So it is, let people be able to define you by your skill and trade and when you dwell upon such a skill, you shall surely prosper and enrich yourself through it.

SO I SAY STAY FOCUSED AND MASTER YOUR SKILL.

CHAPTER

8

UNPROFITABLE TALENT

In all things of nature there is something of the marvelous

Aristotle

"The greatest talents often lie buried out of sight"

Plautus (254-184B)

AFTER THE FESTIVAL, THE THREE FRIENDS AGREED TO MEET AT THE HOUSE OF ANTONIO IN A SYMPOSIUM WHERE THEY SHALL ALL LISTEN TO WHAT WAS WRITTEN IN THE SCROLL BASILEUS GAVE TO THEM

He also had slaves to himself and lived an average life of an Athenian citizen, though been a merchant himself the trade had not profit him much but these days, ANTONIO has been meeting with THE RICHEST MERCHANT IN GREECE and that has began influencing his thinking and way of life. A harsh man to his slaves has now become more friendly and calm; a man who never misses the house of the courtesans at night has now reduced his visit to the city harlots and cheap win sellers.

ANTONIO has become more conscious of riches these days than anything else and has started taking steps to be free from the bondage of lack and wants. Tonight he sits anxiously in his house waiting for the arrival of his two friends Anakletos and Patios whom they were working towards financial freedom

ANAKLETOS: "The content of that scroll Basileus gave to us had been on my mind since the moment we left his place, please ANTONIO unseal the scroll and read the content unto us"

The Rich Scroll

AND THE SCROLL WAS UNSEALED AND ON OPENING IT, ANTONIO DISCOVERED IT WAS A STORY

"My friends, it seems it is another story from Basileus himself" said Antonio

PATIOS: "Okay then, go on and read it unto us"

AND ANTONIO BEGAN READING THE STORY AS THEY LISTENED ATTENTIVELY

...

There once lived a very skilled painter who always ran out into debt, he struggled to feed his family and make ends meet. Tonight he had to rush to a good friend for rescue...

Amir my friend, please can you borrow me a silver coin? I have nothing at home to feed my family with tonight and the gods have not favored my craftsmanship. Said Kazim

"Well my friend Kazim, I understand your plight perfectly, but unfortunately, even the silver coin you asked for, I do not possess but why not ask Kabir, he has been a good friend to us and also one of the richest merchants in Kazuk."

Kazim: "I know of that, but I borrowed three silver coins from him the last time and had not yet paid back. It is two merchant days now; I doubt he will lend me anymore"

Amir: "No Kazim, Kabir is not like that. I know of a friend who owed him 20 pieces of silver coin and could not pay until after six merchant days and Kabir did not bother asking him a penny. Your family needs food and I think Kabir is the only generous merchant that can help you out"

Kazim: "well, it is okay then my good friend, I shall see him tonight and I pray he favors my request one more time"

And that evening, Kazim went to see his old friend Kabir at home.

...

Kabir has become a very successful merchant and lives a life of envy to many. He grew up as a childhood friend with Kazim, but Kabir was not able to afford the formal education at the temple. Although he started but left it to learn trade by following Merchants on the sea day and night in order to master the business. After 12 years of learning, he was able to start his own business of pearls and other precious stones.

Working for others

When Kazim arrived at Kabir's house, he had to wait for a while in the waiting room while Kabir rounds up his meeting with other prominent merchants of Kazuk. As Kazim sat down, he kept looking around at the splendor of Kabir's wealth.

Kazim (thinking): "How I wish I am as rich as Kabir, he has a rich house, a ship on the sea, lovely and healthy kids, and beautiful wives. Every day he keeps increasing in gold, and can travel to any city he desires, and eat anything he wants. His influence has attracted the prominent people of Kazuk to him. O! why has the gods not favored me as my friend Kabir, now am here again to borrow from him a silver coin just to feed my family tonight."

When Kabir was done, he walked into the waiting room to meet his childhood friend Kazim

Kabir: "My good friend Kazim, it is nice seeing you today, to what honor do I owe your visit"

Kazim stood up in respect to greet his childhood friend, who is now a very rich merchant in Kazuk.

Kazim: "My good friend, I hope you won't get tired of me that I wary you too much, for I am a man with lean purse and have come once more to ask of your kind assistant for a silver coin so I can feed my family tonight"

Kabir:"Hmmm, Kazim, that is not a problem to worry about, I shall help you definitely but I get worried each time you come asking for a silver coin. You're a good painter, why the challenge with money?"

Kazim: "Well, my good friend it seems the gods have not favored me yet and the people of Kazuk are not interested in paintings, sometimes I have to give my paintings at a much more cheaper prize to get something to feed my family."

Kabir: "I see, very well then, I also have been thinking about you and wanted to present an opportunity to you"

Kazim: "Really?! I am very ready for anything"

Kabir: "Can you work with me?"

Kazim: "Work with you? That will be a honor but in what way if I may ask? "

Kabir: "I just thought, since your paintings are good but people don't buy, can you paint for me and I pay you?"

Kazim: "Wow! That will be great! There is no problem to that. I can work with you very well on this, it is like a help you rendering to me"

That night, Kazim and Kabir had an agreement and negotiated on how much each painting will go for. Kazim was very happy and said to himself, "Alas! The gods have finally smiled at me". He agreed to sell each painting for 5 silver coins and Kabir gave him freely the silver coin he wished to borrow.

Maximizing Opportunities

The next merchant day, Kabir then bought 2 of Kazim's best paintings for 10 silver coins and traveled with them to Misia, a city very far away, Merchants cross two seas to get to Misia. So, only the rich get to travel from Kazuk to such a city as Misia. It was the center of Art, Artist everywhere, and painting was the order of the day. Kabir had merchant friends in Misia who were into selling of Paintings, so he gave them the two paintings for sale and they sold each painting for 60 silver coin. 10 silver coins went to them, and Kabir uses 20 silver coins to travel to and fro Misia. Kabir is left with 90 silver coins profit after removing the 10 silver coins he paid to Kazim for the paintings.

When Kabir returned back from Misia, he was very happy of the profit and called on Kazim the next day

Kazim has been living happily with his family ever since he supplied Kabir with two portrait of his painting. Out of the 10 silver coins Kazim got from selling his first two portrait to Kabir, he gave his wife 2 silver coins to buy new clothes for herself, he used 4 silver coin to buy food for the house, and 2 silver coins he spent on himself drinking and eating hot red meat with friends at the night merchantry, the left 2 silver coins, he later spent also on his desires.

...

When Kabir got home, he separated his 90 silver coins profit into different parts. 10 silver coins he gave to the temple priest who blesses him, 20 silver coins he gave to the money lender who lends money to other merchants on profit, the money lender returns 3 silver coins as profit for each 10 silver coin given to him after each merchant day. Kabir then put aside 15 silver coins for the next painting he'll be buying from kazim, 20 silver coins for his next trip, 10 silver coin he saved, 5 silver coins he gave his servants to share, 2 silver coins he added to the money he saves to lend those who came to borrow, 6 silver coins he gave his wives and 2 silver coins he held to himself. Then he sent for Kazim.

Kazim: "Evening Kabir, how was your last trip"

Kabir: "O! my good friend, the trip was great and the gods have kept us from the storms of the sea. How about you? How is your trade and family?"

Kazim: "We bless the gods, everything is going on well, I came as soon as you sent for me"

Kabir: "Yes Kazim, I have some work for you to do that is why. I need you to make me three good paintings; one should show the image of merchants on the sea trading; the second should portray the image of the god of wisdom (Madur) and the third should be the image of the king of Lanur. Can you do it?"

Kazim: "That looks demanding but I can. When do you want them?"

Kabir: "The next marchant day, because I will be traveling"

Kazim: "No worries then, that means I have seven days from now to paint"

Kabir: "Yes Kazim, and if you paint well and am impressed, I shall reward you with 4 more silver coins"

At the hearing of the reward, Kazim was very excited and couldn't wait to get out and start painting. As they concluded and he was about leaving, Kabir called him back

Kabir: "Here is 2 silver coins, to put some a smile on your wife tonight"

Kazim: "O! My good friend, you are so kind and generous. May the gods keep increasing you, Thank you a lot"

That night, Kazim visited the Merchantry and enjoyed the wines and red meat before getting home on an empty purse.

...

In the next days to follow, Kazim started his painting day and night with great motivation, he burned the lamp into the darkest hours of the nights and on the 6th day, he was able to complete the work and brought it immediately to Kabir. When Kabir saw the paintings, he was so marveled but covered up his much excitement within. He then gave a brief comment on the work and paid Kazim the agreed 15 silver coins and added the 4 silver coins he promised but made Kazim understand that it was also because of his dedicated time to meet up with the dead line.

...

Kabir took the paintings to Misia where his other merchants were waiting for him (for he has sent words to them about certain paintings he will be bringing). The Painting of Merchants on the sea making trade he sold to the society of Misia Merchants and they valued it for 80 silver coins. The painting of the King of Lanur, he presented it to the king himself who was so impressed to see his image on painting (the best of its kind) and the king valued it for 130 silver coins. The painting of the god of wisdom (Madur), he sold to the temple of Misia and was valued for 95 silver coins. At the end, Kabir was able to realize 305 silver coins which was equivalent to 3 gold coin and five silver coin. The sale was so huge and the buyers were so impressed. Those who saw the work called upon Kabir and asked him if he could paint for them. Kabir agreed and never declined anyone who asked for paintings.

He got their contracts and traveled back to Kazuk where he met his friend Kazim the artist for more work. This was how Kabir made a lot of money from the paintings of Kazim and Kazim was so grateful to Kabir for sparing him 5 silver coins for each paint work and some of the 4 additional coins reward he does get for a good job. Kazim lived a normal comfortable life by working for Kabir. He never crossed the sea of Kazuk for any other city and so he lived and finally died with no inheritance for his family but hundreds of paintings in Misia and other far away cities that he never saw. AND THIS WAS THE END OF A MAN WITH GREAT TALENT WHO PROFIT NOT FROM HIS GIFT, READ ANTONIO WITH A SIGH OF MISFORTUNE.

CHAPTER

9

MONEY: THE GOD-SLAVE

As a slave works tirelessly for his master, so ought money in the hands of its possessor. Money itself takes a dual form; it becomes a slave to those who have mastered it and a god to those whom it has mastered.

So what did you learn from the scroll? Asked Rich Basileus

And Antonio brought out a piece of writing where they wrote their thoughts and presented it to Rich Basileus for consideration.

He read: "The riches of a man are tied to his gifts and potentials but if he lacks the wisdom to draw out the riches from his gifts, he will remain impoverished or another man who is wiser in drawing riches from others will exploit him to enrich himself. And for Kazim, it was a tale of an unprofitable talent."

"Very true, you said it rightly, a tale of unprofitable talent. And many living in ignorance have lost it into slavery and the enriching of others, this reminds me of one of Aesop's fables on the cock and the pearl it says: *"A COCK was once strutting up and down the farmyard among the hens when suddenly he espied something shinning amid the straw. "Ho! Ho!" quoth he, "that's for me," and soon rooted it out from beneath the straw. What did it turn out to be but a Pearl that by some chance had been lost in the yard? "You may be a treasure," quoth Master Cock, "to men that prize you, but for me I would rather have a single barley-corn than a peck of pearls" The moral of the fable holds that;* "PRECIOUS THINGS ARE FOR THOSE THAT CAN PRIZE THEM"

Money exist in dual form

Now I tell you friends,

As a slave works tirelessly for his master, so ought money in the hands of its possessor. Money itself takes a dual form; it becomes a slave to those who have mastered it and a god to those whom it has mastered. It is a slave and at the same time a god and mammon. But to the wise, money is a slave.

Since money takes the form of a god, it only takes the godly nature of a man to control it, for the flesh has no power over money and is incapable of resisting the temptations that comes with it. If a man is first rich on the outside (material possessions), he will be enslaved on the inside (his mind, will and desires) and if a man is first rich on the inside, he will enslave all the riches that is on the outside. He will become a god over possessions, for what he now possesses is incapable of possessing him. The power lies in your ability to transfer the money from your mind into your pocket and not from your pocket to your mind.

Money and its secret

There is a secret about money, he continued; and that is, *"money is never enough"* if a man gains a penny today, he will want to gain two tomorrow and even more every day. You cannot get enough of money, you can only try to be contended with what you get, for as a man grows in status

91

so does his needs and desires; and being contended does not mean a man should stop his quest for more riches, but that whatever he gains in his quest, he should appreciate and create the time to enjoy it without allowing greed to take hold of his desires, he becomes mindful so that his desires for riches will not hurt others or enslave him.

Greed

But the un-contended man never creates time to derive peace and happiness from his profits, the more he gets the more greedy he becomes and the more greedy he becomes, the more desperate he is to accumulate more wealth without minding how many people get hurt in his quest for riches. Greed is not good, but to the evil and ruthless, it is.

Aesop also narrated a beautiful fable about *The Goose With the Golden Eggs,* he said, *"One day a countryman going to the nest of his Goose found there an egg all yellow and glittering. When he took it up it was as heavy as lead and he was going to throw it away, because he thought a trick had been played upon him. But he took it home on second thoughts, and soon found to his delight that it was an egg of pure gold. Every morning the same thing occurred, and he soon became rich by selling his eggs. As he grew rich he grew greedy; and thinking to get at once all the gold the Goose could give, he killed it and opened it only to find nothing. Greed oft o'er reaches itself.*

Quick and easy riches breads greed easily. And the god-money feeds on the greed of men in order to outgrow their power over itself. When it has outgrown the control of a man, it enslaves the man and puts him in perpetual pursuit of riches without satisfaction, it makes such a man addicted to the love of money that he becomes helpless where ever money is involved – This desire can make him do anything for money.

It is my desire on the other hand that you should all know that man was not created for money but money for man and until a man sells his authority unto mammon, he cannot be controlled by the desires of gold and precious stones of the underworld.

Every penny is a slave

Every penny is a slave to its master and every master must learn how to put every penny to work for him. The secret is not that the master works for his slave but for the slave to work for the master. If a master begins to work for a slave, then there must be a transfer of authority, for it is only authority that differentiates the master from the slave. You must learn to make every penny work for you and not you work so hard for the penny. The rich man is just a person, but behind him, there are hundreds of people working tirelessly everyday under his name to make him richer everyday and they may not know it. For example, the man works for the money first and if he is wise, he would later quit working for every penny and start using what he has accumulated so far to establish himself. He may desire to use his money to feed people and still get richer, this man would buy a piece of land and hire people to cultivate it and later harvest it and then sell it to the people who buys it at a profitable price for him and he prospers more.

Now, the money he puts into this venture is like a seed planted to the ground. A man short of vision will only see a seed and nothing more, but a man with a greater vision will see not just a seed but a tree in that single seed which could grow and produce more fruits with more seeds in each fruit and when those seeds are replanted over and over again, it will result into a plantation or a forest full of abundance of harvest for the man who has patiently relied and nurtured that one seed to become a plantation or a forest of abundance.

Wealth takes time and patience

A man who desires riches must be patient enough to accumulate it.

Wealth takes time and patience to accumulate. The impatient man cannot make good fortune. It takes time to accumulate wealth because within those times, life will offer you great lessons and teach you also how to multiply wealth greatly and keeps it growing without depreciating.

At the start of youthful pursuit of wealth, a man is first blessed with time but no money, out of this time, he is expected to create money, and the first 25 years of a man is mostly blessed with time but no money. In these years, he is expected to use the time he has been blessed with to acquire skills and learn how to prosper in life; if you see a man at 50 who is still drawing water from the stream to sell and earn a living, he has not really spent the first 25 years of his life to gather sound skills and knowledge that would take care of him at his 50. When a man has learned the art of prosperity, he begins to apply it to make money in the next 25 years of his life and by 50, he is expected to have grown very prosperous in life and the rest 25 years (Around 75 and a little more for fortunate men) he is to use the wealth he has acquired over the years to take care of his health, give back to the community and prepare himself for the world beyond (he is at this old age expected to be retired and live off on the riches he has accumulated so far). In these three stages of his life, a man Learns, Earns, and Spends. Only a few live life; many just exist. My concern is not only that you may learn, earn, and spend wealth, but that you will also live life to the fullest.

Many chase after riches and forget to enjoy it and also to bring up a good successor that can maintain and increase the wealth they have left behind.

The Goldsmith and the money lender both understand the value of a penny, so also the money changers and the treasurer. They do not underestimate how profitable a single penny can be, so they treasure every penny and are accountable for every coin that goes out of their purse.

Money begets money

The golden rule is that gold attracts gold, money begets money. The rich attracts more riches and get richer every day, they circle themselves with the rich who present to them rich opportunities that makes them richer. With these connections, they penetrate the high places in life and turn things to their favor, and the ungodly among them manipulate the law and corrupt the system because of greed. Money does not know who is good or who is bad, it goes into the hands of the man who can attract it and the man who understands it the most and can persuade it the most wins the biggest portion of riches on his side.

We all know that riches flows through both good and evil channels and the riches that is accumulated through evil comes in great abundance but with great troubles and the riches which comes from good carries within it contentment and a peace of mind. A man must chose first what channel of riches he does want and how much sacrifice he can make to acquire such riches, but he must bear in mind that no one has yet been able to cross to the world beyond with his riches.

SO MY FRIENDS, I SHALL BE TRAVELLING FOR A LONG TIME BUT BEFORE I LEAVE I SHALL STILL TELL YOU ONE MORE STORY AND DEMAND OF YOU A TASK TO BUILD YOUR OWN WEALTH UNTIL MY RETURN.

CHAPTER

10

THE SCRIBE

Nothing captivates the rich like integrity: with integrity a man can build himself an empire of riches and abundance and not fall

"Where there are friends there is wealth"

- Plautus (254-184BC).

I N MY PURSUIT FOR RICHES, I was given many scrolls to read about riches and these scrolls contained the tales of many men who become so rich and others who lost riches to vanity and misfortunes, their stories thought me great lessons and also fashioned my thoughts and guided me in the accumulation of riches. I tell you stories because you can easily remember these secrets you have learned when you recall such stories; like a picture, they speak a thousand words. So my friends listen carefully to the story I am about to tell you and open your eyes to the secrets hidden in it, for these are your keys to a prosperous life.

Here is one of the stories that helped me greatly in using my abilities to profit both myself and others, and I desire it helps you also.

WE ARE MUCH READY RICH BASILEUS, FOR WE EAGER TO LEARN THESE SECRETS OF YOURS AND YOUR WORDS HAS INSPIRED US GREATLY. PLEASE SPEAK

Chasing after money

Yes my friends, I shall speak but first when I was in my quest for riches, I was advised not to chase after money for money chases only after fulfilled ideas and when I have the idea and fulfill it; then the money will find reason to chase after me. Until a man fulfills an idea, he should not remain contended for an unfulfilled idea, for it is as useless as an unfulfilled thought.

Now, here is the story my friends.

There lived a man called Hadar, who lived his life holding unto one key word. INTEGRITY

He observed that in the City of Edom, people hardly trust each other. So he set in his heart to live a life of integrity and trust worthiness. He pays his tax as due, serve each master he was under with both diligence and loyalty, when he works on a grain field he charges less than others do, he attends the synagogue and also volunteer in cleaning it. Hadar denied himself the wines at the night stand and tries to make friends with key people in power.

Whenever Hadar visits a friend, he goes with a little gift (these gifts he gets are common and inexpensive gifts but the receivers attach great values to such gifts because of the love that comes with them – other times, he get gifts for a friend's little children). Hadar not only used Integrity but also love to win friends.

...

Before all these, Hadar was not even an indigene of Edom and his name was not Hadar but Raz. He came from Ai and in Ai, life had been very miserable to him. The opportunities were slim and himself was a lazy man, he goes out for menial jobs, collecting rotten foods from homes and taking them to the pig houses for few shekels and then spending it on drinking at night stands and comes back home dizzy and then sleeps off until life awakens him up the next day.

Raz lived an unserious life until the day he met Aliza, a beautiful young Lady and daughter of a very rich man in Ai. It took Raz two years to woe Aliza but her parents rejected the relationship because Raz was neither rich nor from a rich family. As time goes by he tried to be responsible but no one took him any serious until he came up with an idea after talking to a friend. His friend adviced him to become rich for only in this could he win the heart of Aliza's parents. Then Raz met with Aliza in secret and engaged her without the knowledge of her parents but each promised to keep themselves for each other after which they agreed on their love and then he took off to Edom for another life with a promise to come back for the love of his life.

Building Reputation

In Edom, no one knew anything about Raz, so he took up a new name and called himself Hadar (meaning glory and splendor). He studied Edom and observed that integrity was rare, so he decided to be a man of integrity and furnished it with love and knowledge. Hadar worked hard at peoples farm, took care of their sheep, did other laboring jobs (some down to the nights). He reduced his sleep and stop drinking completely (it wasn't easy on him but he was out for something). He got himself a nice purple cloak, and began making friends. He suppressed all his unhappy and sad feelings and always puts up a happy smile for everyone, his aim was to gain friendship and trust and that he did. He made friends with both the low and high and kept in touch with them as he worked hard in secret places and uses the money to get gifts for friends, lend them if they are in need, and get a free lunch for most. These acts of love made Hadar one of the most loveable persons in Edom.

Raising Capital

After two years, Hadar had gained both trust and love from all his friends and then he set out for what he wanted.

He paid a visit to his good friend – The Temple treasurer at his house

Temple treasurer: "O! my good friend Hadar, you are welcome once more to my home, and thanks for your gifts, my two little girls loved them, they talk about you a lot and are much happy seeing you. So, how have you been?"

Hadar: "I am doing well my lord"

Temple treasurer: "of course, for the smiles never goes off your face. So to what honor do I have your visit today"

Hadar: "Thank you my lord, I have only come to pray for your noble assistance and do hope am favored"

Temple treasurer: "O! That is good then; to what can I be of help to you? For you have been a good friend and have never asked me for a favor"

Hadar: "Yes my lord, I need to start a business but do not have sufficient capital and need about 200 shekels to start with"

Temple treasurer: "200 shekels? That is quite a money and I do not have such unless the temple's money but if am to assist you from it, you will have to give me your word for the refund, for that is the most I can do because you are a very good friend and of great integrity"

Hadar then agreed to the Temple treasurer's terms and promised to refund it the next year and the temple treasurer agreed to the terms and lent him the money.

Using the relationship he has established with some of the prominent men of Edom, he was able to borrow two thousand shekels from ten prominent men promised them on different times of refunding, and then set out to Jerusalem. None of them knew he had borrowed money from the other.

...

In Jerusalem, Hadar already knew what he wanted and at his arrival, he got information about the city and people who were already into the kind of business he wanted to get into. The business idea Hadar had in mind was that of a Scribe. Jerusalem was into a revolutionary period in history where philosophy, religion, and the art were the order of the day. The Scribes were making a lot of money from copying and recording of documents. It was mostly the rich and average that could afford their services.

Hadar knew that to get a group of Scribe to work for him was impossible for he is neither a scribe nor knew the people much, so he took another route. He met a Scribe who had retired from the craft and negotiated with him. Scribes were paid 30 shekels for their work but Hadar promised to pay the retired scribe 60 shekels if he could work for him.

Using the experience of others

Jehu: "Your proposal is very good Hadar, but I wonder what you want me to do for such a huge amount"

Hadar: "It is a simple thing I wish you to do for me and that is to teach and train some young men for me in the craft of a scribe, for am in need of them"

Jehu: "Is that all you paying me for?"

Hadar: "Yes my lord, I am afraid that is all I need you to help me with and I shall remain grateful, for I wish to empower 70 young men on the skill of the Scribe"

Jehu: "That is not a problem sir, when do you want me to start? For I am retired from the King's service and do not have anything doing"

Hadar: "You can start as soon as I get the young men my lord"

Building a company

After their agreement, Hadar offered a job opportunity for 70 young men to be trained informally in the skill of the Scribes. He did all these in secret and used his house as a training ground for the young men. He made an agreement with each of them for a three year engagements before they are free to leave the job if they wish and they all agreed for they had nothing to lose: They will acquire the skill and will be paid for using the skill.

When Hadar got the young men, he called on Jehu who started his Job to train these young men informally in the skill of the Scribes. He poured out all his experience of over 30 years on the young men, for he was verse in the skill and has worked for many people. And after six months, he was through with his job and was paid in total 360 shekels for the consecutive six months which was really huge money.

Hadar then rented a big house which cost him 250 shekels as the work house for the 70 Scribes. He divided them into different sectors which included: Politics, Religion, Education, Philosophy, Entertainment, Secret works, and History. He thought them on Integrity, love, and good relationship with the customers and then opened the Scribe house by inviting some prominent people of Jerusalem to launch it. On that day, Hadar made a free work for everyone who came and informed them that the cost for common works is 6 shekel instead of the normal 12 shekel people pay for a common scribe work. And with this, Hadar began having people bringing in their works for copying and documentation and Clients were treated with so much love and appreciation that they always leave smiling and satisfied.

Secret for successful Business

Hadar thought his workers on good communication and attitude when with client and not to promise a client to come for a complete work on a day they could not finish. Soon, People with top secret jobs started bringing their works for copying and translation which cost more and Hadar already had a group handling secret works. As time goes on, He began monopolizing the scribe works in Jerusalem and before the year runs out; he has realized about 20,000 shekels because of the 70 men's man power used against just one man power of a scribe. There was great division of labour and works were done more accurate and faster, people did not need to wait for two weeks or more to get their works, they could get it within a week and at a cheeper rate.

Paying back

After two years, Hadar was able to pay off his debts and became so rich among the Scribes of Jerusalem. It was after all these that he went back to Ai to meet his love. On his arrival, no one knew him well, for he entered the city with an entourage of 40 Camels and dressed in purple cloths. The parents of Aliza could not believe when Hadar introduced himself as Raz. And with his present status, he was able to marry Aliza and reward his good friend who advised him at first. This was how Hadar (Raz) became one of the richest scribes in Jerusalem.

NOW, 14 years had passed since Hadar started the scribe business in Jerusalem and had the 70 men working for him. Some left, many stayed, and many more joined them. This made Hadar one of the richest men in Jerusalem at that time, but before these long years and at the start of the scribe house, Hadar did many interesting things worthy of note.

He never had the legal right to establish a Scribe house, for he was not a citizen and much more a scribe and was not a member of the scribes of Jerusalem. Hadar made it possible by utilizing what he can for he knew that if a man does not have what it takes, he can liberally use those who have what it takes to get what he wants. He made great negotiations with the retired prominent scribe, Jehu. He established a loving and trustworthy friendship with Jehu and then requested of him a friendly favor, for it was through Jehu, a registered and well experienced and connected retired scribe that Hadar secured a permission to start his business, first using Jehu influence.

Stream of income

It was Jehu who stood by him and opened the scribe house as if it were his, for Hadar by law could not open or do a Scribe house business because he neither was a Citizen nor a Scribe. Jehu went as far as winning the hearts of many clients to Hadar's Scribe house and ensured he got access to woods, papyrus, scroll handles, ink, and all the tools needed before handling the business fully to him and base on their negotiation, Jehu requested for nothing more but a percent of the income of every work done as his share on the business. Hadar agreed to it, for one percent was nothing big and enlisted Jehu a percentage of every work done and through this, Jehu also prospered as a retired Scribe without doing any work for the rest of his life. Be it when he was awake or asleep, money rolled into his purse every minute of every day.

For everyday, the 70 scribe do more than two to four works a day, so he gained above 140 shekels in a day and even more.

AND BASILEUS TURNED TO HIS FRIENDS TO SEE THE LOOKS ON THEIR FACE BUT THEY WERE ALL LOST IN THEIR THOUGHTS, MEDITATING ON THE PATH HADAR TOOK TO ENRICH HIMSELF.

So my friends, once more you must find a reason to succeed and a determination that has the power to take you from a zero to a hero, and from nothing to something. You must have a WHY for riches and that WHY must be strong enough to keep you all throughout the difficult times in the process of making riches.

And lest I forget, do not be so negligent in life to the detriment of your own fortune, for many have wallowed in miseries because of their negligence. Among the scrolls I was given to read, I also encountered and interesting story of an UNFORTUNATE SCIENTIST

CHAPTER

11

THE UNFORTUNATE SCIENTIST

It is better not to have an idea than to have one and not utilize it

L ong time ago here in Greece lived a man named Drazelius.

This was the time when knowledge was scarce and science was emerging. Philosophers were working hard to find the explanations for everything: why the sun falls and rises, why a woman is different from a man, why we die, why people fall sick and many questions disturbing the hearts of men.

Drazelius was a young scientist who was one of the pupils of the Practitioners of the Hippocratic medicine. He had been trained to know the human body and how it works. He on the other hand was a very curious and passionate man who spent most of his time in his laboratory trying to find out about new things.

A discovery

One day, Drazelius came across a plant (permafume) which to him looked desirable to the eyes and special, so he had an unusual bond with the plant. The plant was deep red in color and grows very conspicuously amongst other plants. It was known by many but was never considered by any.

...

Anthonio: "Sir, what do you intend to do with this plant you found?"

Drazelius: "I know not Anthonio, but I desire to enquire of anything special from it"

...

In Athens lived another thinker named Tobit, who was trained at the Aristotle Lyceum and was a very passionate and desperate scientist himself, and who for his curiosity and findings was well known and respected by other philosophers of his time.

...

Drazelius began his work on Permafume alongside Anthonio, his assistant. When working on the plant extract, they discovered exciting things about it. The plant had healing powers. It could heal wounds very rapidly and could be used to reverse the effect of poisons. The discovery was highly rewarding to Drazelius that he decided to keep it to himself for a while that he might be sure of his findings.

Unprotected ideas

Tobit been a distant traveler, paid a visit to the region where Drazelius lived. And when he was there with friends, he overheard of Drazelius discoveries about the plant which was only disclosed to few, then after his visit, he went straight to Athens which was the center of Science at that time. Tobit then went and found the plant (Permafume) and introduced it to other scientist around, he told them he was working on the plant to find out its curative abilities. This excited most of the scientist around and they gave him their support. Tobit rushed his experiments and discovered same result as Drazelius, he found that by mixing the plant extract with other chemicals, you get a good scent and the plant could clean up skin wrinkles. Tobit was so excited and went immediately to report to the Society of Science about his discoveries and with proper confirmation, the Society gave Tobit the patent right and founder of Permafume.

When ideas are delayed

Now, Drazelius finally concluded his work and set out with his Assistant to Athens in order to report to the Society of Science about his findings, but when he arrived, he was met with the greatest disappointment of his life. The Society told him that this same plant has already been worked upon by another scientist and all the properties discovered by Drazelius, the scientist has already discovered them and even more. Infact, Drazelius was accused of trying to steal Tobit's findings without referencing him as the founder. All these made the unfortunate scientist so miserable and disappointed. His work has been stolen and there was no way he could prove them wrong and claim his work. Both him and his assistant had no clue what had happened.

Commercializing ideas

Tobit, after his discovery of Permafume, began making portions of it and selling at a very high price for everyone who desires it. The permafume was very irresistible to many for it had so many unique functions and the most fascinating is making a person look younger by removing the wrinkles off their body. When Tobit realized how much people were demanding for it, he then set up a structure and employed people whom he taught the magic formula used in preparing the portion so he can produced more in little time. And with this, Tobit became rich from the discovery of another man.

...

Before Drazelius could realize the truth behind everything, Tobit had already made great grounds off his discovery and had secured the patent right for the product. It was a miserable end for Drazelius and his Assistant, for they had worked a whole year in wasted effort. Tobit on the other hand, kept adding new things to Permafume and making different product from it like portions for healing injuries, portions for youthfulness, and portion for scents and beauty. He supplied not only Athens but went as far to other cities to market his portions which people bought in large quantities. And the more Tobit became rich, the more frustrated Drazelius was and so eventually, Drazelius gave up the ghost in regret.

Beware of thieves

There are thieves in every profession and a man who does not know how to secure his treasure or delays in achieving them shall be robbed by a more desperate man. Every idea you conceive has seeds of wealth in it, and no idea is useless. Drazelius had the idea, he worked on it but he delayed it and did not protect it firmly, he took it as a casual routine just like his other experiments.

Everyman is looking for an easy and faster way to get rich and this desire to get rich drives many to desperate actions, so you must guard your treasure with all your heart, you must act as fast as you can on the ideas that comes to you before you regret having it in the hands of another man.

Commercialize your ideas

A man should not only be interested in discovering new things in the world, he should also be concern on how to convert his ideas into something tangible, useable, and money making. This is the beauty of ideas, that they can be translated to profitable ventures. Think! It is good for a man to think but a greater part of thinking is how to commercialize your thoughts, for what is the profit of knowing so much and possessing very little? It is unprofitable. Ideas come to a man not just for him alone but that through him others may gain and bless him with their substance. Idea is not enough to make a man rich, he must know how to commercialize that idea to thousands of people.

I BELIEVE YOU HAVE HEARD MANY STORIES FROM ME, SO I SHALL DEMAND OF YOU TO START BUILDING YOUR CASTLE OF RICHES AS I TRAVEL AWAY.

CHAPTER

12

SAVE TO MULTIPLY

"Worthless people live only to eat and drink; people of worth eat and drink only to live"

Socrates

"Rich Basileus, how then do we start to create our own wealth, for you shall leave for many days and we do not have the much skill to make money?" asked Patios

BASILEUS: "No Patios, you do. You now have the necessary skills it takes to make fortune. With all I have said to you before now, I have revealed to you many ways by which a man can grow rich...

Wealth creation

BASILEUS: "My friends, this great city of Athens was named after the goddess of wisdom, Athena but in it you still find men with great wisdom thriving on lean purses. I do not call such wisdom in itself, for true wisdom enriches its possessor in person and in purse. But many of you who desire gold soon fall asleep at the ninth hour of the night and awake not at dawn but when the sun rises in full, and then walk to the Temple of *Ploutos* (the god of wealth) praying for riches you earn not.

In my early years as a slave

I worked under a very rich Master for seven years and while serving him, I learnt so many things about the life of the very rich. My Master, Bishak had grown very rich that he dominated the rest of the wealthy merchants in Persia. Many a times was he accused of been greedy and a monopolist but those were his dominating forces in the market.

My Master started like every other merchant in Persia, he spent most nights telling us about his adventures and how he became wealthy. *"It is no secret to get rich"* he will always say, a man only needs to be smart enough and ready to take the advantages that comes his way and also create some for himself. Every idea is important in getting rich, and there are no useless ideas, for it is out of these so called useless ideas that so many people have become rich in surprising ways.

There was a night when he sat us under the night moon and told us of his little beginnings: "I started life as a brick layer," he began, "and in those days, we worked very hard under the heat of the sun for just a little penny a day"... I was young and full of energy and can do all sort of menial works. I make bricks, I do carpentry, I fetch water from the stream, and I worked in several farms just to make ends meet. I had never thought that an ordinary man like me could become rich. In fact I had never thought of getting rich myself; life's misery had a great toll on me that I could think of nothing else but only how to get the next penny in order to eat.

I could not get myself a wife because I had no money to keep a woman, and many were we in this same shoe that had no privileges of enjoying the basic things of life. The best we get is admiring the exotic dishes on the rich man's table; we will stay anxiously waiting for the remains of meals and drinks. When we see a rich man passing by, it is like a god passing and many times, we envy them because they seem to enjoy all the good things of life and leave us to wallow in misery.

We do discuss amongst ourselves saying, "The rich know not suffering at all, they have never worked half a day under the sun and all they desire they get, they do not know pain or misery, and do not go hungry for a day. We will spend many of the times criticizing the rich, and blaming our parents and blood lines for not been rich because if they had been rich, we wouldn't wallow in such poverty and work so hard for just a little penny. Life was just work, earn, and eat. Nothing more

WHEN MY MASTER SPEAKS OF THOSE TIMES when he wallowed in extreme suffering and poverty, he talks in anguish and regret, wishing he knew what he now knows about getting rich. He will say, "Ignorance is very evil and highly destructive. It enslaves a person in utter darkness and misery. The worst is when a person is in ignorance and he thinks he is in light, that kind of person can never learn the truth nor be set free from his ignorance." Then he continues, "I was in complete darkness and knew it not. My friends too were no different from me; we all think alike and do the same things to survive. They were no better than me and in fact I thought myself as the smartest amongst them, so, I dwelled in misery because of my ignorance."

We sat listening to him as you are listening to me today and we sympathized with his lot. None of us ever thought that our Master had suffered such extreme poverty in his life time; we thought he had been rich and had riches passed over to him, so we were all amused and thrilled by his story.

Work to get rich

Then he will continue and at this point, a beam of smile always radiates from his face whenever he reaches this part of his life story: he will say, "And one day, when we were working under the heat of the sun, a young and wealthy master said to us, 'I see how hard you work every day and later spend all your earnings on food and drinks and the common pleasures of the average man, why not work to get rich than work to get food?'" we all laughed at what he said because we've never heard such words and they seem meaningless to us for we thought, how can we work to get rich in this impoverished situation we are tied down to, but later that night after the day's work when we went out to spend all that we had earned on food, drinks, and pleasures, a thought struck me when I was about to eat, the words **"work to get rich and not work to get food"** these were the words of the young master we laughed at. That night before I slept, I pondered on those words, "work to get rich and not work to get food" and it sounds reasonable, and for the first time, I could not sleep but began to desire riches I knew not.

A step to riches

The next day I was at the house of the young master who spoke those words and out of sixteen of us, I was the only one who returned to enquire of those words again from the young master and the young master was so pleased when I asked him to enlighten me and show me how I could work to get rich and not just work to get food. Because I was curious and now desired riches, he then volunteered to show me how. He said, **"Until a man thinks beyond his belly, he cannot draw out the riches from his head**; the ways of the poor is only limited by the desires of their belly. He then asked me if I could work for him, and I agreed. My young master was into pearls, fabric, perfumes, and precious stones. I began working for him and he paid me my wage but he used that opportunity to also train me. He paid me 30 silver coins monthly and I was contended with it. This was also about the same amount of money I earned in a month while doing menial jobs, so I managed myself with it.

I worked for the young master for months, and he asked me to just observe what he does. He said nothing more to me, and left me on my own. Still, things were though on me and the 30 silver coins he does pay me, I end up using all for feeding and have nothing left, but since I wanted to learn from him, I decided to be patient and do as he said. I was much older than he was but I never thought of that to mean anything to me, all I needed was a skill and it does not matter whether am older or younger than the person teaching me, I must respect him to get what I want.

When in the market, other people like me working for their masters will say that my master was exploiting me and paying me far less than I deserved. I then made enquiring to know how much people like me earn and I discovered that most of them earn between 40 to 50 silver coin and I got furious with my young master because I thought he was exploiting me too much but I kept quiet and didn't ask him any question.

Raising capital

Now, at the end of the year, young master stepped into my room one night and threw a bag at me and left. I wondered what was it and curiously opened it and to my surprise it was a bag full of silver coins, I was astonished and counted the silver coins carefully, there were 480 pieces of silver coins in that bag! I ran immediately to young master and asked him what the money was meant for? And he replied, "That is your money of course, all of it!" and I was shocked and asked how? He then replied, "Those were all the silver coins saved from your wages" I was confused the more, "but I did not save anything" I replied, "yes you did not, but I saved it for you, right from the start, I had decided to pay you 70 silver coins a month, but to teach you the first lesson to getting rich, I withheld 40 silver coins from you and paid you just 30 silver coins because I knew you may not understand it when I ask you to save and also I knew you could survive well with 30 pieces of silver coins and you needed not more than that a month, so I took the excess from you to show you the first lesson of every rich man. The 480 silver coins you see in that bag is the sum total of all the savings I did on your behalf for a complete year".

That night, I was revealed to the greatest lesson of life – the power of savings. And it was a lesson I subsequently trained myself to master for the rest of my life. My young master made me to save on my own two more years of same amount and by the end of three years of working with him; I had saved about 1,440 silver coins! Something I had never earned nor seen in my entire life!.

Starting a trade

He then used that money and introduced me into the business he had been doing for 20 years and guided me with the knowledge I had acquired from the past four years working with him. I was up many nights working to increase my profit and at this time, food was not my desire, my desire was to grow more richer and prosperous, I did all that my young master taught and asked me to, although I made some foolish mistakes from which I learnt the hard way. Later in life when young master passed away, I took over his trade and managed it for his family and also prospered in mine.

After 10 years of been with Young Master, I had transformed greatly into a very prosperous man, and in the heat of a day, I decided to take a walk down the streets and to my surprise, I still found all the 15 of my old friends still doing what we had been doing together 15 years ago before I decided to follow the saying, **"work to get rich and not work to get food"** some of them tried to hide themselves from me when I came by and those I met in other places felt so inferior standing before me and could not look confidently into my eyes, neither could they talk freely nor hit me freely as we usually do 15 years ago when I was with them. That was when I realized how much young master had transformed my life and that he built an invisible immunity of wealth around me that the ordinary man could not come near me nor relate in an absurd way before me. RICHES MY FRIEND, TRANSFORMS A MAN GREATLY.

The Abundance

Today, I have grown to the extent that I now dominate almost all the Persian market and other merchants are seeing me as a threat and putting forth allegations against me to the law giver that I monopolize the market and should be charged for such unfair action.

But how can I do such? For I cannot chase the customers away, neither can I tell them not to patronize my goods nor for them not to like what I sell."

When my Master talks about how dominating his success had become, he smiles so much and is happy for such a success that keeps others restless and always talking about him. He is actually a fine merchant and understands what the people want and how to supply such nice things at an affordable rate. He sends his ships as far as Egypt and

Babylon to get what the people need and he is so friendly to his customers. Many of them come to buy from him because they always leave with a broad smile.

Winning your customers

He sells not only goods, but also happiness and he had spread that attitude to every one of us working under him, he treated us like friends not slaves and taught us things that a master can never tell a slave. His relationship was so close to his customers that he easily become friends with them, and when those customers go home, they talk a lot about him and how good he had been to them and this draws their friends and relatives to come buy from him. Master understood the simple secret that every merchant ignores and that is, **"The customer is more important than the money".** If you can treat a customer well, you can sell anything to him for any price and he will buy with a cheerful and merry heart and even allow you to keep the change.

Make your product affordable

Master grew very fast and became a dominant force in the market, controlling about 80 percent of the market. He added style to whatever he sells to the people and made it very affordable. And example is that, most of the merchants only sell a whole fabric for 10 silver coins, but master can divide that whole fabric to about five pieces and sell each for 2 silver coins and people will rush it. If a normal merchant sells 6 fabrics a day, Master would sell 12 or more fabrics a day when divided into little affordable pieces that could be bought in a faster rate.

And each time he was taken to the court, the other merchant always lose and no matter what they try to do to cut down his sales, Master always create another way to make his money and still dominate...

AND HIS FOOTSTEPS HAVE I FOLLOWED DELIGENTLY AND TODAY I AM NOW LIKE HIM IN GREECE. I HAVE GROWN MORE RICHES THAT I CAN SPEND AND THE ATHENIANS SAY I DOMINATE THE WHOLE MARKET. I SEE TRULY, THAT IF A MAN DESIRES RICHES, HE SHOULD DO WHAT THE RICH DO AND HE WILL GET THE RESULTS THEY GET.

And my friends,

You have read from the Babylonian Merchants how they saved and grew richer by the day. Although Babylon, a city surrounded by desert and with no water still flourished with the hanging gardens and great prosperity from different nations, many of the merchants who desired riches knew that the first step was to start saving a part of all they earned. Most of them who could not resist the temptation of money gave a part of their earnings to the Goldsmith to save it for them that they may increase.

So my friends, you already have a source of income, for if you had not one, my first task to you would be that you FIND A DAILY SOURCE OF INCOME.

DO NOT ONLY RELY ON THE WAGES OF THE LABOR YOU GET PAID AT THE END OF THE MONTH BUT FIND ON A DAILY BASE HOW YOU MAY HAVE A STREAM OF INCOME FLOWING INTO YOUR PURSE.

Accumulating income

It takes a river to make a sea. But never stop the water from flowing into the river, as it is well said, "drops of water make an ocean" so save my friends for this is your first task and the core habit of every rich man.

ANTONIO: "Do you now suggest we start saving a tenth of our incomes?"

BASILEUS: "Yes I do, for that was the first lesson I myself was thought. And before this, I do not know how to save, I say to myself 'maybe if I start working and earning big money then I would start saving' but it was a lie, for if I cannot master the act of saving with the little I get by the day, then I cannot save even when I earn much. And I discovered that learning to save is not only a way to riches but a life style and a vital habit that separates the rich from the poor. The rich saves while the poor eats everything. If you must grow in riches, you must be a saver of incomes". Wisdom demands you first learn to save a part of your earning AND ONE TENTH HAS REMAINED A GOOD BARGAIN ALL THROUGH AGES"

CHAPTER

13

THE MONEY LENDER AND THE POWER OF INTEREST
To every labor there is an interest

BASILEUS then spoke to them saying, "A man who sought riches must be a good friend to the money lenders so he can understand well how money is used and how interest in gained...

Many of the rich men in the past have made good company and friendship with two sets of people; the money lender and the goldsmith, although most Goldsmith also act as money lenders. They lend money especially to merchants on business for an agreed interest. The question is, how does the money lender gets so much money to lend out?

Be trustworthy

Now, every money lender knows that the life of his business is in trustworthiness and transparency. He has to be accountable for every penny that comes and goes out of his purse and his word should be his bond. When a money lender is found untrustworthy, he loses patronage and his business dies, he also must not be driven by greed but must control his desire for gold.

When the Money lender possesses all these traits and has been tested and trusted over the years to yield greater profit, people begin to patronize him gradually and this increases with his ability to attract prominent investors to his side. He gets his money from all class of people; the rich, the poor, the middle class, merchants, and craftsmen of different professions. Some bring in their money to save while others to invest and the bigger the money the more profit he gets.

Most money lenders we know are goldsmiths themselves, so they deal also with precious metals and have a safe storage for such precious objects. Merchants are very good friends with the Goldsmiths, for they get the goldsmith to make precious stones and jewels for them and also, their money is safe with the goldsmith.

Making profits from savings

When a person comes to save with the Goldsmith, he has very little interest to his money depending on how much and how long he keeps the money. But in the hands of the Money lender, money multiplies every day, each penny attracts its kind. And a man can acquire so much profit by investing his money with the money lender.

The Money lender counts his profits by the days, when he lends out 100 silver coins for 20 days, he will be expecting back 120 silver coins and if the borrower cannot pay back at the agreed day, then the interest keeps increasing as the day goes by and if he keeps the money for another 20 days, the money lender will be expecting 140 silver coins. In most cases, borrowers also have problems paying back at the agreed day, so the Money Lender profits much more from them.

Protect yourself from loses

Now, in fear of compromise and theft or insincerity on the side of the borrower, the money lender has made good friendship and agreement with the law giver and is protected by the law, so he need not drag for his money with the borrower. And before the borrower gets the money, he must present some valuables equal the money he is borrowing should anything go wrong, the law giver can hand over such property to the money lender.

Planning for the future

There was a wealthy Merchant I know of who when he got married was worried about his new born child. He was afraid should he be dead the young boy may not have anything to himself, so he visited the Goldsmith and explained his plight. The Goldsmith understood him well enough and gave him a piece of advice.

He said to him, "Very well my friend, I understand your fears and have just this little advice for you. Get yourself a good law giver and establish an agreement with him then search for a trustworthy money lender and put in the name of your son 300 gold coins under the protection of the law giver and allow the gold coins to begeth itself…"

He said also, "For every 300 gold coin the money lender gives out for 30 days, you get an interest of 6 gold coins and 6 gold coins interest for a year is 72 gold coins, that means, for every 300 gold coins the money lender gives you back, 2 percent of it is your interest (but mind you, the money lender could make an interest of 5 percent which is 15 gold coins but because you agreed on 2 percent, he will give you just 6 gold coins and keep the rest as his profit) but there is an interesting part with the money lender, he also make good profits for people with special request like you who have long time to wait before collecting their money…"

The wealthy Merchant was curious and wanted to know more, so his friend the Goldsmith continued

The power of compound interest

"…after the first 30 days, you gain an interest of 6 gold coins, the money lender then adds up the 6 gold coins to the 300 and that gives you 306 gold coins for the next month. In the next month your interest will be 2 percent of 306 gold coins which is 6 gold coins and 12 silver coins, this will be used for the next month and 2 percent of 306 gold coin and 12 silver coins will be given to you…with this, the gold coin accumulates faster and in 7 years, you must have gathered a very huge fortune with no effort for your son to inherit.

Although many do not know this but there are Kings who after understanding this secret, took it upon themselves to enrich the people. In the Roman Empire, the military designed a special plan for every person enrolled into the army. A certain percentage of the person's earning was save by the government for him and after a period of 25 years in the military service, such a person is paid all of those money and their interest as a retirement benefit, this plan was very good for the common army who has no time to save money, because the government does that for him   but as time goes on, the system was corrupted by the politics and many did not get to enjoy such benefits as they ought to. I tell you this so you may know that such a principle is applicable and is also a long term plan to get rich.

AND ANTONIO ASKED: "And how do we go about that Rich Basileus?"

The law of sowing and reaping

Like a seed of grain, money multiplies in multiples for harvest.

And just like a seed needs to be nourished for it to grow and multiply, so does money needs to be nourished in order to grow and be ready for harvest. The mustard seed is a peculiar seed and very tiny of all the garden seeds we know but as little as it is when planted into the ground and properly nourished it begins to grow but this growth is not instant. It grows very slowly and if the farmer is not patient enough, he will soon give up on the seed thinking the seed is dead and unyielding but a patient master will wait patiently and everyday he will go out there and water the seed with only a great hope. As he waters the seed every day, he is not aware that the mustard seed first begins to grow under the earth, spreading deep and wide in the ground preparing to break through the earth. And after many days of consistent patience and nourishment, the mustard seed shots up out of the earth and at this point, the growth of the mustard seed becomes unpredictable because a lot of energy has been put in building a strong foundation deep into the earth. It is at this point that the patient farmer smiles greatly at his labor of investment.

The mustard seed grows and outgrows every other plant in the gather! It overshadows them all and yields greater returns for its master, the barns are filled with its harvest and in great abundance does it come.

BASILEUS turned looking at Antonio who was in front of him and intently listening and said," That is how money works! It doesn't matter how much little you start with but if only you can be patient enough and nourish that little you have, it will latter bring more to you in the future"

If you want to get rich he said, then you must be very patient because it takes time, patience and a bit of sweat to make money and with great money you can move great mountains!.

CHAPTER

14

WORK TO GET RICH

The belly has impoverished many than enrich them, until a man can control his throat, his labor cannot enrich him

PATIOS: "But Rich Basileus, do you discourage us then from hard work. And if so how can we increase our income without working hard to earn it?"

Basileus laughed heavily

"It seems you are not following my teachings rightly, I did not discourage your hard work, I only discouraged wasted hard work driven by ignorance and lack of purpose, until a man tie his hard work to a goal of a wealthy purpose then can his hard work profit him so much. You cannot replace the place of hard work in the life of the rich. Do you not see how I work hard every day? You may not see me molding the bricks, mining the gold, shipping the goods, or making the linen cloths but I work as twice as all of the people that work for me. They become my hands, energy and feet while I become their brain and motivation.

So you should not be deceived, not because you do not see me work hard under the heat of the sun like the brick layers or sandals makers that means I do not work hard to accumulate wealth. No, don't be fooled by what you see on the outside, for many work so hard than you think when you go to sleep. They stay deep into the nights burning the candles to come up with ideas and solutions you know not of.

Today you may not see me work so hard in person, that is because I had once worked so hard and have accumulated this much and now, what I had accumulated works for me. I pay people to work for me, my strength is now getting weaker and I have so many deeds to handle, so I used the wealth I had accumulated in my prime age to hire men with strength that can do the work I desire to.

Friends, do not be deceived that the rich do not work. A man cannot take away the dignity of labor from riches. It is how diligent he is to his work that attracts the kind of riches he desires.

Take example of Kings. Do you see them in the farms? Do you see them molding or laying the bricks by themselves? Do you see them at the market place selling and buying? Of course not, they sit on the thrones and draw wealth to their kingdoms. They even work much harder than many on the thresh mill. They spend most of their times handling the affairs of men and building a great Kingdom.

You may say the Kings already have people working for them, and that's right. But they had paid the price through a lineage and blood line of hard working men. Take for example when the Kingdom is not yet established. A man must develop himself in the skill of war, he must win battles, he must sacrifice so much for the helpless, he must be able to lead a group of men and followers to victory, he must be able to unite them, he must be able to help them build houses and capture more lands and treasures of other natures; it is in this struggle, hard work, bloodshed, hunger, and persistent leadership that the people now bestow upon such a man the privilege to lead them as their King. And this royalty is what is now inherited by his children's children, and today they sit on the thrones established by sweat, blood, and treasures of the founding King of the Kingdom.

If you work hard today, you can save the seat of your children tomorrow but you must teach them the value of hard work in success, for that was what built your great fortune and power. If you feed them wealth without the skills and wisdom to maintain it, they shall lavish it like a fool and waste everything they had like the prodigal son.

"But Rich Basileus we do work hard and still cannot get rich! For I know of a friend here in Greece who works down the night as a blacksmith but still yet he remains where he is five years ago and is not rich but works very hard. What can you say of such a man?"

What you have observed is true, that many work so hard and earn so little. They sweat day and night with nothing to show for. I do not disagree with you in that, for not all hard work leads to riches because it is not the work that makes a man rich, it is what he is working after that makes him rich. You friend works hard but he does not work hard after riches. You must know where your hard work is leading you to; you must tie your hard work to a bigger goal, a wealthy goal. All your hard work must be running to fulfill an idea. Don't just work hard to earn a living, work hard to fulfill a wealthy course.

Hard work does not make a man rich; it is an ideal goal oriented hard work that enriches a man. My Master passed unto us the secret of his young master, he said to us, "Work to get rich and not work to get food". The poor man works just to get food, he is satisfied with the daily penny that can get him by the day, all he thinks is how to work for the next meal. Anything outside that is sheer luck, he believes the rich are either born rich or are a bunch of lucky people life had decided to choose and bless them above others, but that is not true. Life is a good master and is not unfair, he rewards every man according to the desires of their hearts and the hopes of their lives.

Because the poor only thinks of his daily meal, he works hard and uses the money just for his daily needs, the excess he uses to enjoy himself for the hard work he had done. So, such a man cannot be rich because even when he has much, he has nothing worthwhile to achieve with it. He desires not riches, so he would not think of saving, investing, and doing business, he will not understand that each penny that comes to him can be multiplied, so he will spend all he has and enjoy life and then pray to the gods to provide more for him and elevate his poor state.

The rich minded man works to get rich! His mind is on riches and how he can multiply every penny that comes his way, he is willing to work under the heat of day, to deny his gratification and find possible ways to multiply his incomes. He does not waste extra penny, he also looks out for better skills that can enhance his chances of getting more penny into his purse, he is not stagnant and does not accept the lot that only a select few were destined to be rich.

Do not work as the Bull or the Donkey, the Bull though big and full of strength becomes useless to itself; it profit only its owner, the Donkey goes wherever it is pushed to go, it carries quietly whatever load put on him and works all day profiting very little or nothing at all. The Bull is taken to the farms to plough and work so hard under the heat of the sun with a bridle on its mouth so it cannot eat from its labor. Work like the lion, the lion has a mind of its own and does not work for anyone. He is very bold and confident of himself and although not the fastest, strongest, largest, or wisest of the animals, he still rules over them all as king. The elephant fears it, so are the fast gazelle, and the wise serpent. The lion teaches a man of self confidence and the ability to enrich himself even in his deficiencies.

THE RICH FACE EACH DAY AS LIONS WHILE THE POOR FACE EACH DAY AS COWS

He continued, "On one of my journeys, I was very impressed with a young man I met, we were discussing at length with him on many subjects and he seems verse in knowledge but at a point in time, he interrupted and said to me, 'Basileus my good friend, do you know I am a potter?' and I said No I don't and he began telling me about his trade and what he does and how far he had gone, he also took me around and showed me most of his hand works and I saw that they were beautiful and very impressive and with no further thought I asked if he could supply samples of his potteries to Athens, for the people of Athens loved potteries and used them a lot, and he agreed and supplied me samples of his work and when I presented them to my friends, they rushed the potteries and requested for more supplies from him and this was how we became friends with him and most of the potteries I supply to the prominent Athenians were designed by him.

You may wonder why I decided to share this story with you, it is but to enlighten you that a man must make known his gifts, discipline, and craftsmanship to others. In simple conversations, you should not be shy to tell others what you do, be confident of your skills and discipline and accept the realities of things, for many times in this race, you shall be the sole representative of your business, so you must be able to market yourself well enough and you also market your products.

I discovered that people don't buy things but buy names. Suppose we both sell plates of same quality and we both have different sales room carrying our names, people will rush to buy from me because they saw my name on the sales room and they know ho I am, that I travel a lot and bring the best of things from faraway lands but on the other hand, people may patronize less your goods because they hardly know such a name or a person, although we all are selling the same plates but they will tend to buy more of my plates than yours because in their minds, my name stands strong and reliable to them than any other name. as such, your task is also to make a good name for yourself and make that name go as far as you can and make it sound from the lips of everyone you can and let them know what that name represents and by so doing, you shall lessen your labor and profit more from your name and product"

AND ALSO, YOU MUST KNOW THAT THERE ARE STILL RICHES WHICH CAN BE GOTTEN FROM MULTIPLE SOURCES, AND BASILEUS ASKED OF THEM TO COME WITH HIM

CHAPTER

15

MULTIPLE INCOMES

The best source of income is many incomes

Variable investments

AND THEY WENT OUT TO THE FIELDS, Basileus owned a very large garden where he grows different spices and supplies a majority of Athens, he also rare fowls, goats, sheep, and Carmel and sold them for meat and as beast of burdens.

PATIOS: "You have a rich garden Basileus, is this all yours and for your household?"

BASILEUS SMILED AT HIM AND REPLIED, "No Patios, although my household benefit from my gardens but it is a means of daily income"

PATIOS: "But you are already a merchant of jewels, pearls, and grains, why also stress yourself with a garden or are you not contented with what the gods have blessed you with?"

BASILEUS: "Hmmm, young Patios, of course I am very contended with what I do have and to be contended does not mean a man should live with little but that whatever he lays his hands upon and profits from it be it little or much, he should be happy and grateful to his creator and also enjoy all that he has profit but if he allows greed and ungratefulness to creep into his heart then he will not value what he has and even if he has much he would wish for more thinking by having more he will be happy but the more he gets the more greedy he becomes and would not have a peace of mind from his abundance.

Multiple sources

And to your response Patios, you must understand today that there are no limits to acquiring wealth and the more sources a man can create for wealth the richer he becomes. The very rich do not depend solely on one source of income; they find ways to create multiple sources outside their primary source of income. Take me for example, you know me as a merchant and that is my primary trade and I make a lot of money from it but I also have a garden from which I sell spices, fruits, and vegetables to others, I am also a states man I hold a post as a trade adviser in Athens and I am paid for that, I have blacksmith who make Armors of war for me and I sell to the Athenian Army, I rare camels which I hire to travelers and also sell to those in need, I have houses in Athens for rent and also little *Stoae* for relaxation, I deal with lands and properties and also I have goats, cattle, and fowl for meat and all these bring daily income to me outside my trade. I have so far over 12 different sources of income outside my primary source as a merchant of jewel, pearl, and grains. And these other sources of income has enriched me more than I possibly could imagined and as the day goes by, they keep expanding and bringing in more profit to me. Most times I just sit down and listen as my workers tell me how much money comes in everyday"

ANTANIO: "Hmmm, wise Basileus, you have indeed mastered every step of prosperity under the sun, none of us had such insight to acquiring riches, our labor is focused mainly on our trade and we see such activities as a distraction to our prosperity in what we do"

BASILEUS: "The average man sees only his primary source of income and everything else a distraction. Have you seen the men who work for the state? Most of them depend solely on the state and their wages, they have no other sources of drawing daily income, so they depend solely on the state and before the month runs out, they must have spend all their wages before it is been paid. They keep borrowing and promising to pay back when they get their wages, but the rich think differently and do not depend solely on the wages of the state, they find ways to create other sources of daily income no matter how little the money may be, and if a source brings in a drachma a day, and they have about seven sources, that is seven drachma a day and almost the daily income of a physician. And these daily incomes will keep them from borrowing or in the bondage of lack"

ANAKLETOS: "So then Basileus, if we must do what you now say, will it not cost us much time and energy? And how do we go about it?"

BASILEUS: "Well, if your focus is on getting rich it will not be a burden to you trying to increase your chances of accumulating wealth by creating multiple sources. Although it will take away a little time and effort but in the later, it will be worth it

Multiple sources of income is a fast way of accumulating wealth and so if a man can, he should think of other ways he can make money outside his primary source which may limit him in many ways"

AND OUTSIDE HAVING A MULTIPLE SOURCE OF INCOME, A MAN CAN ALSO GROWN FORTUNATE BY INHERITING RICHES BUT RICHES THAT ARE MERELY TRANSFERRED ARE CHALLENGING TO MAINTAIN WHICH IS THEIR TRUE TEST, AND BECAUSE OF THIS, I SHALL TELL YOU OF RICHES THAT WERE INHERITED BY MEN.....

CHAPTER

16

TRANSFARABLE WEALTH
Build wealth for others

I n ancient Babylon, children of wealthy parents cry rich at the death of their parents.

Most of the wealthiest people outside the royal families and merchants gained their riches through the inheritance of their parents. Some force their parents for the share of inheritance even before death. And this was how many young men became rich.

Once was a very Nobel and wealthy man with daughters and sons born to him, he had servants both males and females bought to him from different cities. He had over 500 camels, thousands of sheep and cattle. So great was his possession that his children lacked nothing. They wear the best of cloths and party together with friends and families, there was nothing they desired that they did not get.

The power of loyalty

Now, in this noble man's house, the servants lived separate lives of service and dedication and amongst them all was Coos. He was born a slave to the noble man and was bond for life as a slave, this fate he took in good faith for he was from the Jewish lineage and was thought by his parents on the virtue of stewardship to the master. His parents were captured and enslaved when the Great King Nebuchadnezzar conquered Jerusalem and brought the slaves of war to Babylon where noble men priced them for over a hundred pieces of silver coins.

In this period, Babylon was very prosperous under the reign of King Nebuchadnezzar and wealth flowed through the city despite its deserted region. Merchants came from different cities of the earth to make trade and buy goods from the Babylonians especially the slaves and spices and precious jewels gotten from war. A master could resell his slave if he so wishes or finds the slave untrustworthy. Now, in the house of the noble man before Jehoth was born, his parents were loyal and true to their master. They served him with all dedication and honesty that he was impressed and favored them beyond other slaves, in the act of sincere service; he made Eleazar the slave father of the born slave Coos head over other slaves and also his house properties. It was the custom of some wealthy people who had no time for their homes to hand over the care of their homes to the most trustworthy servant and face other official duties. Eleazar believed in the Jewish God and work in uprightness according to his belief, this made him more dedicated and loyal than the other servants. He won not only the masters heart but became an adviser to him on many issues of life, for Eleazar had wisdom within him

Training up a successor

Eleazar got married to a slave of his kind and begoth Coos as a born slave to the house of his master. The Master favored Eleazar and his family and gave them a comfortable room to live in his house. As the years rolled by, Eleazar took his time to bring up his Child Coos in an upright manner, he took him along to make trades for the master; he taught the little child how to increase the master's assets, all that Eleazar knew he transferred immediately to his little child not minding his age. Coos will ask his father questions like *"why do we have to serve the master?"*, *"why are we slaves and poor?"*, *"how does a man become rich in life?"* So much were his questions and his father never turned any question down or asked him to stop asking questions, in fact he took the questions and used the answers he knew to teach his child on liberty.

He will say sometimes to his son, *"we serve the master so that some day we also can become masters to others and be served rightly; to another question he will reply, we are slaves not because we are poor but we will be poor if we remain slaves even within us"*, and the child will reply *"But we have nothing father and poor people do not have anything"*, *"No son, we are not poor because we do not have material things for now, a man is poor when he has lost all hope about the future and is incapable of finding ways to reach his destination"*

It was through times like these that Eleazar ceased to impact wisdom to his child. Despite they were slaves, Eleazar believed that if the mind of a person is flooded with good thoughts, it is just a matter of time and that person will be liberated through his thoughts, for even the ancients believe that as a man thinketh in his heart so shall his ways turn out to be.

Many duties were they that Eleazar did for his Master and on such a day, the master asked of Eleazar how he may reward him, and Eleazar said "My Lord you have been gracious to me all these years and I am favored to serve under your good will and mentorship, I have lacked neither food nor shelter nor water because you provided me with all I needed and if you insist I must ask for a thing then I ask not for myself but for my son; that if you so wish and can be kind enough to watch over him as both a servant and a son unto you after am long gone, I shall remain grateful unto you even in the tomb. This is all I can ask for, if you desire me to ask of anything.

Eleazar request pleased his master considering the fact that he asked not of perishable things as gold and silver nor did he ask for his own freedom but took first the thought of something more important – A lineage and a sustained legacy. This moved the master and he agreed to look into it as a favor unto his most loyal servant.

Now, on the other hand, the master had many children who had no interest in his business affairs. They only needed him when they need something from him, and because of their lack of interest in learning the family business, their father handed them to Eleazar for anything they wanted. He said to him, "Do not withhold from them anything they ask for". He gave Eleazar such responsibilities because he himself was not always around to foresee his family. He was a very busy man, so he made sure he gave the children all the spoils they needed for he believes that all he has worked is for his children to enjoy of it and not suffer like he did when he was of their age.

The Children spent a lot of the money on great luxury and pleasure, all they focused on was to have fun of everything life could offer, and Eleazar did exactly as his master instructed, he withheld nothing from them.

As time went, Eleazar took time to teach his son all that he knew about the masters business; How to buy slaves and profit more from them – He'll say, *when you buy a slave buy them with a smile and make them feel they are now safe in your hands and they will serve you better.* In the grain field, Eleazar will show his son how to make a hundred bountiful harvests and the kind of crops that yields great return, and when they profit more, he will take his son to the money lenders where the master gave part of his profit for investment. Coos had no idea why his father does all these but it was interesting to him and his father was inspiring for he showed him great love and mentorship.

After many years of service, Eleazar passed away and as the master promised, he took Coos as his own son and servant. Coos in his youth had gathered so much wisdom and knowledge of the family business that the master had no choice but to make Coos take over his late father's position, and Coos impressed the master beyond expectations. He served with all honesty and dedication and brought great increase to the master. Now, the master was aged and about to die then he called all his children and divided his inheritance to them all. Deep within him, he prayed that his children would someday have someone as loyal as Eleazar and his son Coos. The master on that day, set Coos a freeman and no longer a slave, that was the best he could do in favor of his loyal servant Eleazar and then he passed away.

Taking up Responsibilities

Some days after the master's death, there was great confusion amongst the children as almost all of them had no idea on how to maintain their inheritance and each began to sort after Coos for his service. Now, Coos is a freeman and could make decisions to be respected by anyone, for he was no longer a slave. He then made an agreement with the children to have ten percent of any profit he will bring to them and they quickly agreed for they had nothing to loss and moreover, they had no interest on anything but that they have what they want anytime they needed it. Coos began working for all of them and supervised the slaves, farms, cattles, camels, gardens, sales, lands, and properties once owned by the master. The work was as usual to him for his father had taught him all he needed to know and even the secret things about the master that the children knew not. As time goes on, Coos remained patient and began gathering his profit from all his works, he worked for about fifteen years for the children and by then, he also grew wealthy from the works of his hands.

A day came and Coos met the children individually and told them he could no longer continue in their services then he left and began life as a freeman. He then started focusing on his own properties which he had acquired from his 15 years of service to the masters children and he grew rich very fast. His camels and cattle gave birth easily as he knew when to mate them and how to care for them throughout their gestational period; he also bought servants to himself, and bought farm lands. He increased everyday he lived. On the other hand, the children of his late master began having difficulty in taking care of their inheritance and had no much experience on how to profit from them, they only cared for what they wanted and they went to any length to get it. Some of them began selling out their properties and when Coos heard that they want to sell a property, he then send a loyal servant of his with a nice purple cloth, a carmel, and a bag of silver and gold to buy the property, the servant acts as if he was buying it for himself and when he succeeded with it, he used his masters signet ring on the papers and took it to him. Coos paid a little more sometimes to buy the properties and with time, almost all his late masters' properties became his and the children were drained of everything, they became poorer with every day that passes by and depended on others to live for the days ahead. Coos prospered with everyday and later possessed almost everything his late master had except the house the children lived in.

AND THIS IS HOW THE DELIGENCE AND WISDOM OF A SLAVE AMOUNTED UNTO RICHES.

17

HIS RICHES: HER WEALTH

The man's riches is the woman's wealth. A woman is as be
autiful as the riches of a man can make her to be in love

ON ANOTHER DAY WHEN THEY MET WITH BASILEUS

Financial plans after marriage

BASILEUS: "Patios, I learnt that of all you three you alone have not yet found yourself a wife , why so?"

AND THEY ALL LAUGHED FOR PATIOS HAD MADE A LOT OF TALKS TO HIS FRIEND OF HOW FREE AND ENJOYABLE HIS SINGLE LIFE IS.

PATIOS: Met the question with a smile and responded, "Yes Rich Basileus, I am yet to take a wife for myself"

BASILEUS: "I will love to see you do that for you have come of age and need not keep throwing your money on the daughters of Aphrodite or the hetaerae so you can start shouldering a responsible life"

ANTONIO: "Very true Basileus, we have talked to him on this matter but he believes it is better to be single and enjoy all the pleasures of life without restriction than to be married and trapped in a prison of commitment and responsibilities that gives you no freedom to enjoy the pleasures of life and live as free as your heart desires"

BASILEUS: "Very well Patios, getting married to a damsel is quite a responsibility and can also trap a man when there is no understanding and trust between them but I have observed most families in Athens and discovered that one of the main issues married people struggle with outside trust, understanding, and sex is MONEY··· the man who is rich a nd has a lot of resources to meet almost all the material ne eds of his wife seems to have a relatively peaceful and hap py home except if his duties in the bedroom are poor··· A ND THEY LAUGHED AT THOSE LAST WORDS··· Very true m y friends, but if he remains fit in such area, then he would have money to contend with, and on the other hand, the man who has little or struggles hard to meet up with the m aterial needs of his wife ends up with more bitterness, unh appiness, and a feeling of incompetency as a man"

THEY NODDED IN AGREEMENT and Patios interrupted

PATIOS: "Then how should a man make his home especiall y for a young man who is yet to take up the duties of a hus band"

BASILEUS: "Yes young Patios, this was why I talked you int o your singleness. We all know that Athenian women are mostly confined to their houses and have little or no role t o play in the society except a very few and also the class of the Hetaerae, so if a man desires marriage he must unders tand that a majority of the responsibilities lies on his shoul ders and must plan ahead of time for Money itself empow ers a man to be responsible. It gives him the confidence to be the head of the family and dictate how things should go .

···

When I was about marrying, I had no sound advice on my f inance so I had to learn out of experience and when I saw t hat the lack of money is the cause of so many friction and argument in marriage, I decided that I shall learn of it and f ind ways to resolve it so I can better advice the young cou ples who intend getting into the marriage union.

I discovered a profound truth about riches in marriage and that truth was, "The man's riches is the source of the wom an's wealth" also, the woman is like a Goldsmith unto the man where he invest his treasures in order to get great val ue, pleasures, and good returns, but on the wrong soil, he regrets all the time, energy, and money he had invested in the relationship.

Another truth is that, it is the presence of a King the transf orms an ordinary woman into a Queen, when a King takes a wife, she becomes his Queen but when a Queen takes a husband he is not so easily called a King but a mere compa nion. The lady may arise from the poorest of families but when she is married to the king, his riches becomes her we alth; and she is adorned with the most expensive and beau tiful of cloths and jewelries, and a royal crown is bestowed upon her to signify how powerful and influential she now i s over the kingdom.

Patios got a little confused and asked

"What do we then now make of these sayings my lord ?"

A wrong reason for love

BASILEUS: "Yes, you can make a lot out of it. First, do not l et the wistful passions of love make you drain away your ri ches, do not try to impress the woman with dazzling riches and material wealth without reason, sincere love should sp ring from the heart and not be attracted entirely by the sel fish gains of riches, for when your riches gain wings and fly away, there will be nothing to bind your love together. Ma ny men have gone insane after burning out their money in the name of love and later discover their lovers have absco nded with another man or becomes uninterested since the re is no longer money to drive the relationship going but w hen the money comes, she tries to show her love again, yo u must run away from such insanity young PATIOS for man y of us have fallen into such a trap and went through so m any heart pains in order to get over it.

The passions of love you must know becomes addictive ea sily, when you get stuck into it, it drains all that is in you in return for little pleasures and affections, such a relationshi p is liken to that of a pest feeding wholly on its host, and t hey become a liability to you and a burden you struggle wi th each day of your life. If you want to be rich young man, you must be prudent with your finances and not allow em otions to dictate how you spend your money, if a woman i s a liability to you, you should cut your expense and invest it on a valuable course.

ANAKLETOS: "But Rich Basileus, how possible is it then for a man to win a woman's heart without lavishing her with money?"

BASILEUS: "HMMM, You speak as if you do not know the game men in Athens play and how they have mastered the art of love and sed uction and have devoted their time to study the nature of a woman and her feelings and how to appease her every f antasy, they become to the woman whatever she desires t he most and appeal to her senses, it is like a game played unto them and by this, they toil with their emotions witho ut necessarily having a penny in their pockets. But this is n ot good and I do not advise you to trade upon such a path. Money should not be your utmost achievement before yo u can love; you must not have a lot of money to make a w oman feel loved and happy, but money in itself has influen ce and the power to attract and easily entices a feeble hea rt, it can also be used to spice up a relationship. And a man can spend as much as he can on a woman but he must first be certain of the lady's love and devotion, for spending on a woman is a business of high risk and investment and if a man spends irrationally because he is driven by emotions t o please or impress the woman, he will soon regret when he realizes that his investment is a great lose. The wise ma n knows that you can never satisfy a woman no matter ho w much you pour into her, so he does what he can and allo ws the rest to be. So my friend, be wise and spend prudent ly, for money spent in the name of love is unrecoverable.

Handling financial crisis

ANTONIO: "But Rich Basileus, what do you have to say abo ut the married ones, for we have a hard time on finances a nd how the money is to be spent or used in the house"

ANAKLETOS: "Very true Basileus, just like my wife who is w

ell established in her business and also earns as much mon ey from her trade as I do but she refuses to make contribut ions to the house expense, I hardly know what she uses he r money for because I do pay for almost every expense in t he house. When I talk to her about this, she picks offense a nd tries to be defensive. Most a times, she says it's my res ponsibility as a man, husband, and father to shoulder all th e responsibilities of the house and she can only come in w hen she feels like and not to do what a man ought to do. I have suffered this for a long time and it confuses me a lot"

BASILEUS: "Well my friend, I understand your plight very w ell, and we know that no man can have all the things he de sires from a woman but most things can be gotten when t he two sit down and talk out their hearts. Money has alwa ys been a great problem in many homes, and for you ANAK LETOS, did you sit down with your wife after your wedding to discuss how you should go with your finances?"···No, I did not, I felt it was not necessary discussing such matters because whatever I have is hers and whatever she has is m ine···"Hmmm, very foolish Anakletos, that was very foolis h of you, and this negligence has become the very root of y our problem, you undermined the place of money in your r elationship and assume your wife should understand you i n all things. Didn't the priest ask of you to enlighten your wife in all things? This does not stop on bed alone··· AND THEY LAUGHED AGAIN···It continuous in your everyday lif e especially your finances.

Money issues

A man ought to talk about money with his Lady, and when he sees that she profits well from her skills, he should enco urage her on using her money to take good care of herself and also assist in the house, she may desire to save her mo ney in order to expand her trade or to buy gold jewelries o r the latest of fabrics and make ups but in doing so, the hu sband should make her see reasons and where her income can help in the house. He should not force it upon her but persuade her into it and make her see reasons but if such a man is very wealthy and well established then he has nothi ng to worry about but find ways to support his wife in the r ight trade if she desires to trade but if she desires not and wishes to remain a house wife then he should treat her as a Queen and lavish her with his gold for her duties in the h ouse as a wife and mother are worth his every gold.

 But still yet, after a man's wedding, he should sit his wife down and discuss with her on the importance of learning a skill or using it if she already has one and also to value mo ney and learn how to save, spend, and invest every penny that comes into her purse. This will help resolve many argu ments between them.

A MAN SHOULD KNOW ALSO that he is no longer a single man w ho can spend his money the way he wishes, he now has a wife to look after and a future which they have to pursue t ogether; he has his dreams and she also has her dreams, t he two ought to discuss the dreams before them and how to accomplish each dream.

It can be very demanding and each will have to cut out unn ecessary wants to focus on what they both need and what matters most to them. You may desire a hut to live in but s he desires a big house, she may be comfortable with eatin g a piece of meat for dinner but you are use to having two pieces, she may love to buy new cloths and dresses and yo u desire fresh wine and a strong camel to travel with. Both of you have different needs, so you must sit down and har monize your needs with better ways of achieving both wit hout leaving the other person behind.

AND NOW BACK TO YOU AGAIN ANAKLETOS, If your wife e arns as reasonably as you, you may agree to add up some percentages of your daily income together and use that su m total to accomplish the desires of your hearts. A percent age is better than a specific sum, you see if you earn 30 dr achma a month and your wife earns 15 drachma a month, it will be unfair to demand that each of you contribute 10 drachma each, but on the other side, it will be fair if each o f you decide to contribute 40 percent of your earnings, the n she will bring 6 drachma and you will bring 12 drachma which in total you both will have 18 drachma to accomplis h your monthly goals and the left over with you can be use d for personal expense such as travelling, buying of cloths, jewelries, or wine, and also for offerings, borrowing to oth ers, and other personal needs. This will reduce the friction between you both than having one person solely depende nt on the other or a misunderstanding due to complete de mand of the total income from both.

Although it's proper that both trust their income in one pla ce, for it will make spending easier but this will make both feel trapped because for every drachma anyone wants to s pend he or she must inform the other and this can be tedi ous to the mind, but if you follow what I have advised, bot h of you will still have something in your hands to pursue y our daily needs and something in your savings to accompli sh bigger goals like building a house, getting an education f or your children, buying of slaves, starting a business and many other great works.

And Antonio interrupted with a question

ANTONIO: "But what if one of both is dead, what happens to everything?"

BASILEUS: "That is a good question Antonio, you think dee p and such is good. We see a lot of Athenian women home less and their children run the streets of Athens begging fo r bread because the man is death and left no security for h is family. Every rich and wise man knows that his responsib ility as a husband and father should still speak and rule eve n after his dead, such a man makes plans for his family and begin to save inheritance for his family the very day he ma rries his wife. You are to start saving an inheritance for you r family. A foolish man leaves great debts for his children t o pay while a wise man leaves great fortune for his childre n to profit and ensures that he protects that inheritance fr om been taken away from them.

Securing the future

You can invest a certain amount of money in the name of your wife and children to the goldsmith in order for it to yield profit in many years to come and you can also save an inheritance from your daily income for them and even use part of the money to buy lands and properties in the name of your wife and children so that when your are no more, they instantly become the owners of such properties and you can write down your will after your marriage and keep amending it in the hands of the lawgiver for you do not know the time and day when death shall take you away. Do not think of writing or making a will on your dead bed, it should be a thing you begin to do after your marriage and every time you achieve something new, you can include it into the will in the hands of the law giver and when death takes you without notice, the law giver shall present such a will to the family and protect them from the embarrassment of relatives and friends. And should such a will be tempered, your wife and children already have lands, properties, and trades in their names which no one can take from them

So Antonio, I believe I have answered your fears?"

ANTONIO: "Hmmm, very well wise Basileus and your word s were very helpful."

AND AFTER SPEAKING TO THEM ON THIS ISSUE, HE THOUG HT AS MUCH IF TO TELL THEM WHAT WAS WITHIN HIS HE ART OR NOT, FOR HE KNEW THEY WOULD NOT BE GOOD MERCHANTS IF THEY DO NOT KNOW THIS PART OF HIS LIF E AND FINALLY HE DECIDED TO SPEAK TO THEM ABOUT A

PART OF HIM...

CHAPTER

18

HIGH RISK FOR HIGH REWARD
The higher the risk the higher the reward; no risk, no rewa
rd

Basileus had told the young merchants so many thi ngs about the trade and the path to riches, but ha s reserved a crucial part from them all; he had res erved his failures and losses in the trade and only told the m of the great successes he had experienced all these year s but the truth still remains that there is no great success without great failures, for it is out of the deepest failures t hat the greatest of successes arises. He decided to release this part of his life in order to help the merchants better ap preciate the journey they are about to take.

BASILEUS: "So my friends, we all know that there are neith er successes without failures nor victories without challeng es and so it is in the pursuit of riches. I have suffered a lot of losses in the course of my business and my goods have been snatched so many times by the Pirates, great valuabl es that could make a man almost run mad. In my first expe rience with pirates, I lost almost everything and it took me over three years to finish paying off for the goods, I was co ned on many occasion and lose my goods and money to cr ooks, cheats, and thieves, I have also had my ships wrecke d in the middle of the sea and my goods all sank with no re covery. So many are the risk of embarking on great busines ses and these are the risk a merchant must be prepared to take when venturing into a business; you have to be prepa red for the unexpected, you have to prepare for the risk ah ead of you, sometimes you may end up losing all that you have invested and need to start all over again and run into great debts at the end of the day but these are what make s a great merchant, his ability to take great risk for either a great profit or a great lose. Until you lose, you will never k

170

now how valuable it is to succeed."

THE THREE WERE SURPRISED THAT SUCH A MAN AS RICH AS BASILEUS HAD EVER LOST SO MUCH AND WAS STILL ABLE TO RECOVER AND MAKE IT TO THE TOP

Antonio: "Hmmm, I must say Rich Basileus that your failur es are far greater than we thought but seeing you today, n o man will ever imagine you went through such a great ord eal in order to succeed in life. So what made you took such great risks? For almost all merchants in Athens hardly go d eep into the sea for trade because the seashore was enoug h for them except the metrics that come from neighboring cities to trade."

Benefits of risk

BASILEUS: "Very true Antonio, many Athenian merchants are afraid to go beyond the seashore to make trade because they want to avoid possible sea dangers, so they prefer the *metics* (*foreign citizens that are not Athenians*) bringing in goods to them at the seashore or the emporia (a place of trade for merchants) where they can buy at exorbitant prices and sell it at a large sum. The metic merchants benefits much more because they do not only sell the goods, they also sell the risks involved in bringing in the goods through the sea. The Athenians are afraid of sea dangers and until a merchant is willing to risk as much as the metics do, he cannot profit much from the business. When you look at Athens, you'll also discover that a metic who is not an Athenian citizen will tend to prosper more from his trade or be more fortunate than most Athenians because he risk so much to be in Athens and such passion cannot allow him to be lazy, so he works as twice as a normal Athenian does and risk all that he has to be a successful man in a foreign land.

I studied the life of the metic merchant and discovered tha t his most rewarding virtue is the ability to take great risk, and the greater the risk the greater the reward. Many mer chants are afraid of risk but they do not know that the abili ty to take risk is what makes a great merchant. When I und erstood the sea and the timing of many pirates and how th ey took captive of goods and gold, I tried out different sea routes although lengthy but it was worth the effort, I also s eparated my goods into different ships so I may not lose e verything at once, and I made friends with the commander s to help me get some of the Athenian best armies to go wi th my fleet on important journeys and I compensated the m for their efforts. These were some of the ways I used to secure my goods on high risk and whenever I succeed in su ch journeys, I profit about 10 times the profit made by the ordinary trader in the Agora (the market place) for I becom e a major supplier to many Merchants even outside Athen s and this prospered me. It is my risk that you now see as a monopoly.

...

BASILEUS went on to encouraged the young merchants no t to be scared of taking risk for high yielding ventures but t hemselves must be wise in risk taking and not take foolish risk that will crumble them forever. Many merchants have not made it big in Athens because they have lived a life of conveniences, they feel satisfied with their daily trade and income and make no effort to increase it or add new ones or sell in large quantities to earn more. Many of the merc hants have lived over 10 years doing the same trade and e xpecting greater returns but getting more frustrated every year when their incomes never increases, they spend coun tless of money on goats, sheep, cattle, silver, gold, and inc ense as sacrifices unto the goddess Athena for divine favor s but nothing changes because they are scared of risk takin g and remain solely on the seashore for trade.

The metics had many chances of becoming more successfu l than the citizens of Athens because these set of people c ome into Athens with great determination to succeed at al l cost and do whatever they can no matter how risky it ma y be to survive and prosper in land. Many of them come in with just a bag on their backs but in five years time, those bags are filled with great amount of silver and gold, and go od fortune keeps rushing into their hands without restricti on. They sleep on the sea, dine with pirates, stay awake all night working, deny themselves great pleasures because t hey want to save, prosper and live the Athenian dream. An d for many years, their method of survival had never forsa ken them; determination, hard work, and selflessness – th ey have mastered the art of risk taking to the extent that t he possibility of dying or failing can never stop them.

...

BASILEUS: "Have you taken the time to observe some of the metics around you?"

AND THEY ANSWERED, "Yes we do"

BASILEUS: "If truly you have observed them, you would have learned greatly from them, although not citizens of Athens but they can endure anything or do anything to survive and make a living. They have so much sold themselves completely to their works with no reservations whatsoever to the course of their lives. You have some as slaves in your homes, others as friends, and others as fellow merchants and of the merchants in Athens, the ones that sail through the sea to distant lands are the metics. Such is the risk a man must take to make it in life.

Although attacked by pirates but the pirates themselves are also taking great risk to enrich themselves, so be it for a good or bad course, the ability to take risk enhances the chances of great fortune.

I HAVE KEPT THIS RISK WITHIN ME AND USED IT TO ELEVATE MYSELF IN THE SECRET BUT AM OFFERING IT TO YOU THAT YOU MAY ALSO PROFIT MORE, AND HERE IS SOMETHING YOY SHOULD KNOW ALSO··· IT'S ABOUT THE MEASURE OF A MAN, WHAT MAKES YOU REALLY STAND OUT AMONGST OTHER MERCHANTS

CHAPTER

19

THE MEASURE OF A MAN

A man is as rich as he thinks

W

hat makes a man?

"Two things makes up a man: ASSETS a nd ACCESS··· the wealth of a man is me asured by how much assets he can gath er under his name and how much access and influence he has on both the low and high in the society" said Basileus t o his friends

"But Rich Basileus should a man have enough money to spend, is he not rich then, since money answers almost all things? Asked Anakletos

BASILEUS: "Money at hand does not really signify true rich es. Such money does not increase in value neither can it ge nerate constant income for the owner. When it is spent, it is hardly recovered as such it has no redeemable value. Th e rich spend their money on assets, they value assets far m ore than money kept in the save; the poor will spend every penny on everyday needs and pleasures and cannot delay their gratifications to save and invest the little excess they gain from their every day labor···

What is asset all about?

Whatever can fetch more money for you can be considere d as an asset; the food you eat, the cloth you wear, the wi ne you drink, the hetaerae that satisfy your canal pleasure s, the house you live in, and all the things you consider as s ources of pleasure and comfort are not really assets but all liabilities because they draw money away from you and do not increase your purse with any penny. The poor spend all their hard earned money on these things and wonder why they do not get rich, their liabilities exceeds their assets and they spend more money accumulating liabilities than assets so they keep sinking down with every day that passes by···

ANTONIO: "But Rich Basileus, all that you have mentioned are things that we need every day to live the good life; should we not build houses? Should we not marry? Should we not eat and drink? Should we not relax our senses after a hard day?"

PATIOS: "Yes Rich Basileus, how can we survive without these basic needs of life?"

BASILEUS: "You see my friends, the poor cannot resist the fumes from the wine neither can they resist the redness of the meat or the scents of the hetaerae. The little penny in their purses shouts out to fulfill their every desire for a temporal pleasure; they are short sighted and cannot see beyond their bellies and throats. They give the very excuses you just gave, they say; shall we not eat? Shall we not drink? Shall we not enjoy the reward of our hard work? Of course a man must eat and drink and have the pleasures of life but if he must be rich he must be able to delay his gratification and control his appetite and desires. Not everything the eyes sees it must have, it can be good and pleasurable but at the time of building wealth, such goods and pleasures are not needful.

To grow rich, you must be able to cut down your excesses i n order to increase your earnings.

PATIOS: "How possible then is that Rich Basileus?"

BASILEUS: "   Well, first, do not spend money on unneces sary things. You must be prudent with your expense and h ave in mind that temporal pleasures only leans the purse. Do not allow what you owe others be more than what you own, for it is what you own that sums up your real wealth. You must buy the basic needs of life and do not be stingy t o your health saying you are trying to be prudent in order t o get rich. What I mean by been prudent is for a man not t o spend more than he needs, save the excess of your earni ngs and use it to buy valuables for yourself. Do not use you r savings to buy liabilities; you should not spend your mon ey on whatever will draw away money from your purse, us e your savings to buy properties and lands, buy camels you can rent out and make money, buy slaves that can work an d earn for you, build houses you can sell or rent out to mak e money, get solid gold whose value never goes down, buil d businesses that can profit you more, and work hard to in crease what you own and reduce what you owe···

When your assets enriches you, then you can have the ple asures your heart desires, for the big difference between t he rich and the poor is that the rich spends from his excess income while the poor spends from his basic income. The more the rich spends his money, the more money he gets while the more the poor spends his money, the more he ru ns out of it. Never spend your capital and the interest for e xpansion, spend the very excess that cannot prevent you fr om expanding.

ANAKLETOS: "Well Basileus, what you have said is very tru e but you also speak of having ACCESS, what do you mean by that?"

Gaining Access

BASILEUS: "Yes I said a man needs both ASSETS and ACCESS to b e rich and of assets I have spoken but for ACCESS I shall tell you. You must know that the greatest ASSET a man can ha ve is not in things but in PEOPLE; People are your greatest assets and that tells you to put people first before the thin gs of life; you should not put things above people but peop le before things. Your prosperity depends on how much AC CESS you have on people; the more access, the more conn ections and the greater the chances of success for you.

To have access you must master the art of human relation ship and make yourself friendly, available, and also accessi ble. Make friends with people of many fields; make a frien d with the town physician, make friends with the priest, th e law giver, the tax collector, the carpenter, the merchants , the cobbler, the potter, the goldsmith, the money lender, and as many as you can. Make a good effort with friends in different disciplines in life and contact them once in a whil e to keep the relationship so that when the time of need a rises you can turn unto them for professional advice or hel p and they shall be of great help to you with little or no cos

t.

ACCESS brings to you great opportunities and when you are in trade, you should make known your practice to all your friends so that when they need such services as yours they can call upon you or when they come across a great opportunity in your line, they can make reference to you to their friends because friends listen more to the advice or references of their fellow friends than anyone else

ANTONIO: "Hmm, very well wise Basileus, your words inde ed are full of experience and wisdom, for we are witnesses at your birthday celebration to all these things you are sayi ng, for we were met with all kinds of personalities from At hens; the emperor, senators, merchants, crafts men, law gi vers, tax collectors, money lenders, and a host of them; all seem to be your friends and you were very close to them a ll"

BASILEUS: "True wise Antonio, you indeed have a good me mory and have spoken rightly, for I am close to all of them. I take time to pay each of them a visit, I also buy a little gift for them, patronize them, and make good gestures with th em, and in return, I get most of their contracts and recom mendations. They are very familiar with my various ranges of trades and know that I offer the best of qualities. When the armies want to go for war, the emperor calls upon me and gives me the very task to make bronze shields and arm ors for the army and he pays me in good return, I also sup ply the designer with quality silk from faraway land and th e elites with beautiful pearls and jewels of gold and silver a nd they all recommend me to their friends, relatives and n eighbors and these gives me greater ACCESS to people and with this great access, I accumulate greater riches for myse lf, for greater number of people patronized my goods and the state gives me good contracts also"

PATIOS: "Hmm from what you have said then, money alone does not make a man wealthy?

BASILEUS: "Yes my dear friend Patios, money alone does n ot make a man wealthy, the world may see you as rich but to be wealthy, a man must tie his name to possessions and valuables with which he can dispose later and still get back his money or rent out such possessions to make money on a daily bases. He must invest his money on things that do n ot depreciate in value but appreciates everyday of the year like lands, gold, cattle, houses, temples, and noble busines ses. These are what measures a man amongst his counterp arts; it is how much he own over how much he owes that s ets him apart, how much assets he can accumulate and ho w much access he can have to people who can aid him pro sper more in life that matters. You see kings marrying out t heir daughters to princes of other kingdom in other to hav e a level of relationship and access to the kingdom, they su pport others as allies during wars in order to strengthen th eir bonds and this is exactly what happens in the event of wealth."

Handling sensitive issues

ANAKLETOS: "I also will like to enquire Rich Basileus, for I have friends who were once in this race for riches with me but after they got married, their passion waxed cold and the dreams they had of riches only remained a dream unto them and they could not make a reality of it. what do you think might have caused this?

BASILEUS: "That is a very sensitive issue you have brought Anakletos, for truly many men have been trapped by the e vents of life than they could imagine. And love in its innoce nt form had actually shattered the dreams of many men as it has also build the dreams of thousands. I will like to say t hat a man should not entangle himself with the affairs of marriage until he is fit to shoulder its responsibilities and a lso pursue his dreams in life. Marriage is also a form of liab ility if one of the two has nothing significant to contribute but depends solely on the other. Well, you know very well that in Athens women has hindered from a lot of social wo rks because it is deemed that they remain at home and tak e care of it while the man goes out to source for the daily n eeds and so, a young man desiring riches must understand clearly the responsibilities that comes with marriage and h ow it may limit him for a while if he has no understanding of riches the way he ought to, for if a man marries in ignor ance and uses that ignorance to pursue riches, he will only frustrate himself the more and will see his wife as a great li ability and burden to him.

But I also say of the woman not to be lazy and solely depe nd on the man but find ways she can also help him, Athens has not banned women from using their talents nor from t he everyday trade, the woman should find ways to help th e man and not live upon him as a complete pest or a liabilit y, for that will drag the man into poverty and great misfort une. I say also to the man, there is no need to rush marryin g a damsel for love tarries and waits and comforts and und erstands. Such a man should build himself to a certain stan d where taking up the place of a husband and a father will not limit his abilities but will encourage him the more and give him better reasons why he must become rich and pro sperous on this life, otherwise, what he loves so much will eventually become a liability and burden unto him and dra in the zeal of life out of him"

AND WITH THOSE WORDS, HE SAID FINALLY TO THEM, "M AKE EFFORT TO INVEST YOUR MONEY IN ASSETS AND ACC ESS AND NOT IN LIABILITIES THAT WILL DRAIN YOU INTO P OVERTY AND MISERY"

BE POWERFUL

CHAPTER

20

POWER SECURES WEALTH

"The energy of the mind is the essence of life ···and the wo rst form of inequality is to try to make unequal things equa l "

Aristotle

Wealth without power is terror.

And wealth does not equal power.

WHEN RICH BASILEUS RETURNED FRO M HIS JOURNEY, he discovered that his friends had applied all the lessons they have learned from his teachings into their daily lives and this transformed the m greatly. Each of them desired and made a commitment t o accumulate riches; they sorted after the WISDOM they n eeded to succeed, They saved a part of their earnings in or der that they may multiply, they began to invest in ASSETS and reduce all LIABILITIES, they focus their efforts in produ cing quality goods and gaining the trust of their buyers but still yet, they remained ordinary Merchants with only the s ayings of Merchants.

Though they had gathered wealth from the wisdom of Basi leus, but their hearts began to thirst for something more. People envied them for their riches but they were not fear ed or revered, something was missing that they hardly cou ld figure out. Although they had money but had no control over important matters in Athens and this feeling of incom pleteness drove them again to Basileus

The need for Power

ANTONIO: "Our dear friend and teacher Basileus, we have done all that you had thought us and just as you have said, we are beginning to get the results we desired, each of us i s becoming more prosperous using the principles you have

thought us but as the day goes by, we began to feel some i
n competencies in our hearts and our minds began to desir
e something more than we now have which we cannot exp
lain"

PATIOS: "That is very true Noble Basileus, I no longer
complain as much as I do about money although friends
envy me but I still cannot have a say in the society, a weak
ago a wood cutter rose an argument with me and he had
no respect for me if I had riches or not and even when I
was on the right standing, I could not do much and I
wonder why, for I thought that with my riches such a thing
ought not to happen to me

ANAKLETOS: "And on my side Rich Basileus, I just still felt a
sort of incompleteness as though I needed something to m
ake my riches more valuable in the eyes of others but do n
ot know what to do···so I met my friends and talked with t
hem on this issue and I discovered they had similar cases li
ke mine and we decided to come and see you once more, i
f by reason of your wisdom and experience might know w
hy we feel the way we felt"

AFTER THEIR COMPLAINS, RICH BASILEUS SMILED AT THE
M AND RESPONDED

BASILEUS: "There is nothing wrong with you and what you
now feel and desire shows that you are stepping into the n
ext phase of wealth where only a few wealthy men desire t
o venture into, many who see themselves as rich remain c

ontented with what they have and refuse to hearken to th
e desires of their hearts until misfortune befalls them and i
t becomes too late for them to take a bold step, for the ric
hes they relied upon is now lost and gone "

ANTONIO: "What do you speak of Basileus? For we are los
t in your words"

BASILEUS: "Your heart desires a protection for your wealth
. What you need now is no riches for you now possess it; w
hat you need now is POWER! The power to control wealth,
power to give you a say in the society, and power to prote
ct your riches, and every wealthy man in Athens knows tha
t WEALTH IS NOT POWER!"

AND THEY RESPONDED IN AFFIRMATION THAT WHAT THE
Y NEEDED NOW IS THE POWER TO PROTECT THEIR WEALT
H AND MAKE THEM SIGNIFICANT IN ATHENS, FOR MANY R
ICH MERCHANTS IN ATHENS ALTHOUGH ENJOYS ABUNDA
NCE OF WEALTH BUT HAVE NO POWER OR SAY IN THE SOC
IETY.

BASILEUS: "Wealth is not power, for if wealth were power,
Talys the tyrant who grew to power would have not been
able to banish the 500 wealthiest citizens of Sybaris. Thou
they had great wealth but they could not protect their wea
lth and could not withstand the tyrant. The story holds tha
t Talys seized their properties and then banished all of the
m from the city. It is a great terror to have riches without p
ower"

PATIOS: "I thought that if a man is wealthy he is also powe rful?"

BASILEUS: "No he is not, and that is the mistake assumed by many rich men; they confuse wealth for power. Althoug h wealth brings influence but its influence should not be m istaken by power, for a man who accumulates wealth begi ns to see himself as powerful – No, he is not and if he be w ise he will use his wealth to gain power and be more signifi cant. I believe you have heard of Croesus, Lydia's wealthie st king, his wealth was so enormous that a man could only be as rich as Croesus and not beyond him; in fact he was t he first to introduce the use of coins as currency, his kingd om was filled with enormous gold that he made his coins i n gold and distribute to as many as he desired···

King Midas

We have read in the writings of Herodotus, that Lydia was the first Kingdom to use the gold and silver coin and this w as in the times of the very wealthy King Croesus when the cities of Lydia were built near the river Pactolus which was believed to contain so much gold in it carried from the spel l of the greedy King Midas who requested of the god Diony sus that anything he touches becomes gold, he was warne d but he insisted and when his request was granted, it exci ted him for a while, but as time goes on he became unhap py with the gift as he could no longer eat nor drink, for all he touched became gold, even his loved ones turned into gold. Soon the gift became a curse unto him and he could no longer bear it, so he prayed unto the god Dionysus who gave him the gift to relief him of such a curse, and the god Dionysus instructed him to go take a bath in the river Pact olos and the curse will be broken.

And so he did and was free from the curse, all the gold sank into the river Pactolus where the Lydians lived, and ever since then, the city of Lydia had prospered with so much wealth and gold .

As rich as Croesus

King Croesus reigned over Lydia and was extremely rich, in all the earth all men were compared by wealth to him; a m an could only be "as rich as Croesus" and no more. The Kin g was the first to mint the gold and silver coin and was pro ud of his wealth. He saw himself as the happiest man on e arth because of his wealth, he thought wealth equal happi ness and also wealth equal power until the day he was visi ted by Salon, the Greek law giver and when he asked Salon who was the happiest man on earth, he expected the law giver to mention his name first but he mentioned the nam es of others and Croesus was unhappy and asked who next ? Expecting his name but Salon mentioned another person , and he asked who next and another was mentioned not h is name and Croesus became so disappointed and ask how about myself? But salon replied that a man can only be sai d to be happy and fortunate after his death.

Later, the kingdom of Lydia was attacked and although Croesus was the wealthiest of men on earth, he could not protect his wealth, he could not overpower the army, for his riches could not equal the power of his enemies. He was overpowered and all his wealth taken from him, some said Croesus was burnt up and saw how unfortunate it is and despite his wealth he could not protect himself from a dreadful death.

Alexander the Great

Men of understanding know that their wealth is not strong enough to keep them, so they sought for power but in the pursuit of power, most of them get corrupt and obsessed with it.

During the times of Alexander the Great of Macedon, the P ersians under the ruler ship of its last King, Darius III of the Achaemenid dynasty had remain a great threat to Greece; they had so much wealth at their disposal that they could buy themselves a great army for war and the Greeks were a rising force against the Persians, although they had no m uch wealth as the Persians, the Greeks developed themsel ves not only in wisdom but also in power. A great military r uler and strategist taught by Aristotle himself emerged as a savior unto the Greece city states. Although very young, Alexander the Great was able to team up armies from diffe rent cities of Greece and raised them unto power to overc ome cities of the world. They were not intimidated by the wealth of other nations because they were powerful and it was through this power that they captured the gold, silver, and armies of other nations.

Wealth on its own cannot secure a nation, it is power that secures wealth and as such, every merchant must not only reach out for wealth but for also power, he will soon be as wealthy as his power.

WEALTH CANNOT STAND WITHOUT POWER

CHAPTER

21

THE POWER OF BARGAIN

Everything depends on negotiation; the best negotiator ge
ts the best cuts

"The poor man who enters into a partnership with one wh
o is rich makes a risky venture" – Plautus (254-184 BC)

THE RICHEST MERCHANT IN GREECE – JERRY AMWE

PIRAEUS the City's sea port which was developed during the times of Themistocles and completed during the time of Pericles had its long wall street which connects the sea port to the city. The sea port has become Athens center of commerce with three different harbors; one for merchant ships, the other two for grain ships and war ships. Athenians could not cultivate much of grain because of the rocky nature of their soil so they depend mainly on grains imported from faraway lands, the war ships comes not only with treasures from war but also slaves and the merchant ships go to distant lands to bring spices, linens, black stones, jewelries, pearls, and lots of goods. The port is filled with all sorts of merchants and traders bargaining and selling new goods to buyers. This is where the power of negotiation and bargain amongst merchants is tested.

...

BASILEUS could not make it to Pireaus because his presence was needed at the Bouleuterion (Athens senate building) where delicate issues on Athenian trade were to be discussed, and as a well experienced merchant in Greece, Basileus was always consulted when important decisions are to be taken on trade.

Since Basileus could not make it to the port, he decided to call upon his three friends and commit into their hands the task of buying some goods for him, he gave them the money for the goods and allowed them on their own. The three merchants were not very good in the port trade, they were good at selling goods in the Agora but bargaining at the port was a much demanding process and they wondered why Basileus would chose they assign them on this task. They went with the money and also with their own needs for as merchants they will wish to buy some things in order to sell

...

At the sea port, the young merchants saw so many exciting and attractive goods, some they desired for personal use and others for sale. Patios moved enthusiastically to a pearl merchant.

PATIOS: "Please, how much does this go for?"

MERCHANT 1: Quickly, the merchant observe the enthusiasm and desire Patios had for the pearl and he said "150 drachma"

PATIOS: "150 is too much for the pearl, I shall give you 100 Drachma"

MERCHANT 1: "Sorry sir, this Pearl is from the Phoenicians and one of its kind, I cannot sell the pearl for less than 130 Drachma, if you are satisfy with the price then fine and if not, then am sorry I can't go below that"

PATIOS tried to drag with the merchant but the merchant refused to lower the price and seeing that he loved the pearl so much he decided to pay the 130 Drachma for the Pearl.

They then went to the grain sellers and bought the grain which was for a fixed price and returned home to Rich Basileus.

BASILEUS: "I see you are back early, it means the market was great"

"Yes it was" they responded

BASILEUS: "Patios I can see you bought a beautiful pearl for yourself, so how much did it cost you to get that?"

And patios with a great smile replied, "Just 130 Drachma Sir"

130 drachma? Hmmm, well you can all come in

And when they went in Basileus brought out same pearl that Patios bought and showed him.

"Wow! This is same pearl as the one I bought, so how much does this cost Rich Basileus?"

"70 Drachma"

And Patios exclaimed, "70 Drachma! That means I have been cheated so much"

"yes you have Patios and that is the business people live off life with every day, I presume when you saw the pearl you loved it for its beauty and could not hide your desire for i t, so the pearl merchant noticing your desire and that you will pay anything for it decided to make the best use of the opportunity"

"But I bargained with him greatly and that was the best price he gave me"

"well Patios, I do not say you have not tried in your bargain but next time, to avoid all these you should first carry out a survey price for what you want to buy so you can have an idea on how to bargain and whenever you want to buy a thing you so desire, you should make every effort to conceal out your desire from the merchant otherwise he will feed on it. and when you feel he is been very insistent, always have the courage to step out, and because no merchant wants to lose a sale, how will definitely call you back for a fair price"

PATIOS: "Now I get, I must be very foolish with my bargain then"

BASILEUS: "I wouldn't say that but it was an avenue for you to learn how to master the power of bargain. You see, when you are out to buy a thing, the merchant at first does not tell you the exact price, he mostly tells you twice or thrice of the original price then it is left for you to breakdown his price and start from either a half or quarter of the price he offered, and from there you can begin to bargain by adding very little to your proposed price, and sometimes, showing him the money at hand to make him know you do not have as much as he had said may help him come to concl usion and sell the goods for you"

AND AFTER THEIR DISCUSSION, BASILEUS TOOK THEM OUT TO ONE OF HIS SALES OUTLET. There were people crowded mostly wealthy people and trades men in Athens and some city states of Greece. There were precious goods and paintings in the front of the room with a seller in front of the audience and he will pick a painting and began talking

DEALER: "Here is one of our magnificent paintings today and is the only copy you can ever find anywhere, a master piece which will be sold for the highest bidder and the start price is 80 Drachma"

And after a brief silence, the audience will begin to respond, "85!" another "90!" "Okay, we have a ninety, anyone else?" "100!" "Yes, we have a hundred" someone interrupted "120!" and so they bid until they got the highest bidder at "250!" and the painting was sold to that person.

This was how they sold all other commodities for the day, and at the close, everyone left the hall satisfied and very proud of what they had bought. BASILEUS then explained to the three men what they had saw

BASILEUS: "So, this is another form of bargain you have witness today, the highest bidder goes with the goods, this form of bargain is very profiting most times because a great value is attached to the commodity to be sold because of its rareness or significance, and anything can be sold here for any price and great importance can be attached to anyt hing especially to the properties of great men who are dead and have certain precious belongings"

ANTONIO: "Does that mean the original cost of that thing is not significant here?"

BASILEUS: "No Antonio, of course it is, you see, the man who sold out the painting said something before the start of the bidding, he said, '⋯ and the start price for the painting is 80 drachma' that means no one can bid it below 80 drachma and in the real sense, that painting cost 80 drachma but at the end of the day we were able to sell it three times its original price that around 250 drachma and the buyer was happy to buy and possess it. so this is another form of bargain where what matters most is the value of the thing and people are ready to pay any price for it since it is the only copy in existence or the very few left .

And on this day, the three men were introduced to the power of bargain as both a buyer and a merchant, for the ability to negotiate the price of a thing or win over a buyer was very important to the profit making of every merchant and such skill must be mastered accurately, for when a buyer agrees on a price be it twice or triple the original price, an agreement has been established and the seller is free of every guilt that comes with the profit from such a trade.

NEGOTIATION IS THE ANCHOR OF PROFIT MAKING AND ANYTHING CAN BE SOLD FOR ANY PRICE IF ONLY THE SELLER CAN CONVINCE THE BUYER ENOUGH TO ACCEPT THE PRICE AND ALSO IF THE BUYER CAN CONVINCE THE SELLER EN

OUGH TO ACCEPT HIS PRICE. THE ONE WHO CANNOT BAR GAIN ALWAYS LOSE AWAY TO THE ONE WHO CAN AND SO IS BUSINESS.

CHAPTER

22

PAY ALL THAT YOU BORROW

He that borrows enslaves himself

Borrowing enslaves.

Those who could not pay their debts ended up been enslaved to their lenders, they worked and served the lenders until the day their services could pay their debts.

...

Entangled

Philocles once lived a free and fair life, with his money he could buy whatever he desires and pursue his dreams but when he got married, he could not help but borrow to meet the needs of his family. A honest man he was but the lack of money made him dishonest, he could not meet up with the dates of refunds and so his debts piled up so much that he could not face his creditors who were once his closest friends, he now sees them as enemies, his borrowing has trapped him and since he could not pay his debt off, he became defenseless against them and whatever they say to him he does without any excuse. Philocles life became a web unto him and for the rest of his stay he kept hiding from his creditors and those he could not hide from he was enslaved to and such is the fate of every borrower; they cannot have a good night sleep neither can they have a say in front of their lenders.

...

BASILEUS: "So my friends, it is better to lend than to borro w for he who lends rules over he who borrows, it does not matter for what purpose the money was borrowed. It is an exchange of right and power in that he who borrows subm its his right and power to him who lends, the borrower nee d not say it; his entire being naturally becomes enslaved a nd indebted especially if he has no means to pay back for t he time been. It is funny how we see creditors as our great est friends when we are in need and our worst enemies w hen we are to pay back our debts. A rich man is known by how much less debt he owes and how much more assets h e owns and every rich man will tell you that nothing gives y ou a good sleep than going to bed and knowing you owe n o one."

AND AS HE SPOKE HE RECALLED MOST OF HIS LIFE MOME NTS WHEN HE HAD TO BATTLE WITH DEBTS TO BECOME T RUELLY FREE

In all that you do if you can please avoid debts to the best you can – PLEASE DO, for it is better to go hungry than to g et satisfied with debts, you may end up forgetting you owe someone a little penny but I tell you, the creditor has a ver y good memory of his debtors, he may pretend about it bu t he never forgets he has some money with you and when the debt is big, you begin to hide and avoid your creditor. When I was to start my first trade on pottery, I was excited and went about to borrow money from many friends and when they borrowed me, I saw them as the best of friends but when I started the business and it was time to pay bac k, I began to feel very reluctant and I tell you, no matter ho w much money you have borrowed, paying back seems no t worth it. The money which took me a day to borrow took me months to pay back. I said to myself, 'when I make eno ugh profit I shall pay back' and whenever I meet my credit ors and could not hide from them, I apologize for not been able to pay at the right time and promise to pay another d ay and so it was that my debt became my greatest evil and if I must prosper, I must   settle every penny I owe, for that was my first step to a free life.

PATIOS: "Your debt must be great then and we wish to kn ow how you Basileus were able to settle all of these debts and still prospered"

AND BASILEUS MADE A GREAT SIGH BEFORE HE RESPOND ED

Paying off debts

BASILEUS: "My debt, I had to pay every penny with my sw eat. I didn't find it an easy task for I must pay for the food I eat, the cloth I wore, the shelter I live in, and my other nee ds. I had no such learning about growing wealth as I now r eveal to you so I suffered a lot of difficulty; I said one night unto myself that *you must pay every debt you owe Basileu s* 'then I wrote down all my debts and to whom I owe ever y penny. I started from the largest debt to the least and I di scovered that my debt were so much than I thought⋯ a m an will look down on his debt until the day he writes down every penny he owe and then he'll discover how much he must pay⋯ my debt was about 700 Drachma"

ANTONIO: "Hmm, a huge debt it was. Tell us how you settled your debts"

BASILEUS: "I was ignorant in settling of debt like I said so I kept quiet and decide to work hard in order to pay, I started with the largest debts and so I struggled and every penny I get I took it to the Money lender for I had borrowed about 300 drachma from him but as I paid him bit by bit, I got frustrated until one day I discussed the issue with the Priest and he said, 'No young Basileus, it is a foolish way to settle your debts, you forgot all others and frustrate yourself with the much. Now tell me, which is your least debt and to whom and how long?" and I replied, "my least debt is a drachma I borrowed from a friend to eat and it's a week now " "good, then start with your least debts and when you are done then I should know" so I went on and started paying off my very least debt and I discovered that it was more easier to pay a drachma or two than to pay 300 drachma and for each drachma I paid off, I earned back my friends whom I thought as enemies and some of them surprised me and asked me not to worry when I approached them with the one or two drachma I owed them and so I was relieved.

But a day came that those I owe 20 drachma and above started bothering me, one came and told me he must get his money before the sun set so I was confused and had to go and borrow 10 drachma from another friend to pay him off and I was relieved for a little while and so I did with the next person I owed 20 drachma.

How to pay off huge debts

And on the day I came to the temple, the priest asked me, "So Basileus, how is your debt now? Have you paid the littl e ones I asked you to?" "Yes I did teacher, it was much eas ier to pay a drachma than to pay 300 drachma" "good, an d how about the other debts what are your intentions?" th en I replied, "Well teacher, I still struggle with that and I hi de from creditors, the other day one came nagging me so I had no choice but to go and borrow 20 drachma to pay hi m" "Hmmm, young Basileus, when will you learn that borr owing money to pay a borrowed money does not resolve t he debt, it may buy you time and a little relief but the debt still remains; all you did was to transfer the debt from one person to another. Well, you must learn, and so must ever y fool, now you have seen how easy it is to pay little to sett le a debt and still meet your daily needs, now let me ask yo u, 'have you talked to your lenders about your debt?'" "N o I have not, I wanted to have something at hand before I meet them"

"Hahaha Young Basileus, you indeed speak childish; you o ught to go and speak to everyone of them and agree on ho w much you can pay each of them and still have something to keep to yourself, you cannot please one lender because he gave you the largest sum and forget about the others, it is not wise; if you can, and I suggest that you carry them al ong" "But I do not understand your sayings teacher"

"How much do you make a day Basileus?" "I make 3 drach

THE RICHEST MERCHANT IN GREECE – JERRY AMWE

ma a day" "good, so in a week you will have 21 drachma a nd in a month about 84 drachma, right?" "Yes teacher" "g ood, now tell me, how much debt are you left with?" "abo ut 600 drachma, 300 for the money lender, 50 to the jewel seller, 100 to a friend, 60 to the Goldsmith, 50 to the Temp le treasurer, and 40 to the potter" "Hmm, that is good, no w here is what you can do, from the 84 drachma you earn a month you must sacrifice 34 drachma (about 40 percent) of it and every month you use that 34 drachma to settle yo ur debts until you clear them all but first you must follow e ach of these men and explain to them what you are about to do and how you intend to settle your debts with them a nd show them the list of debts you owe and where they fal l on your list and when you can possibly pay each of them. " Then I asked him, "How do I then go about all these?"

And he replied, "You can start with two or three of them a nd I suggest you start from the least on your list, if you pic k the potter and temple treasurer, you can split the 34 dra chma between them with each having 17 drachma to hims elf and in three months you will settle the two then pick th e jewel seller and Goldsmith and in three months you will s ettle both, then pick your friend alone and in three months you will settle him then last pick the money lender and in nine months you will settle him and by so doing you will cl ear your debts and be free but if you keep running from yo ur debts and not plan ways to settle it, you may live with it for more than five years, so Basileus, go and write down yo ur debts then talk to your creditors on you intend to pay th em all and when they should expect their money and then

start working towards that by putting aside a part of your i
ncome for debt.

BASILEUS: "And so I did and agreed to work for a monthly
pay and not a daily pay for I shall spend it easily if I was pai
d daily then I wrote down my debts and followed all my le
nders showing them my list and where they fall and how a
nd when I intend to pay them all and to my surprise they w
ere pleased with me and were now relaxed knowing that I
will definitely pay them and when I would pay it. I started
with the least to the largest and in two years I paid my deb
ts debt and so I became free from debt and had the friends
hip of my creditors back, in fact some of them didn't not c
ollect their complete pay for they were impressed by my a
ctions and were touched also so they asked me to forget a
bout the remaining debt"

ANAKLETOS: "Rich Basileus, I must say you are fortunate e
specially meeting with the priest, his advice was simple, ap
plicable and less stressful, for after removing 40 percent of
your income you still are left with 60 percent to meet you
daily needs so you would not borrow again and by followin
g all your lenders and discussing with them on how you int
end to pay them, you would not have to hide from them a
ny longer nor have a sleepless night because of your so mu
ch debt"

BASILEUS: "Very true my friend, I was now confident to m
eet them at the market place and smile with them and wh
en I had paid the first two, they were impressed because t
hey knew their turn will come suddenly and I need not bor

row another money to pay anyone, although it was not eas y adjusting to a lifestyle of 60 percent of my earnings but I felt it was worth it and in no time I shall be free from all m y debt and then start building my asset. I tell you, if you do not desire to lose a friend then don't borrow him money, i f you have enough give him freely for money in the hands of a friend creates guilt and separation."

AND THIS WAS HOW YOUNG BASILEUS FREED HIMSELF FR OM THE MENTAL SLAVERY OF BORROWING AND WON BA CK THE TRUST OF HIS FRIENDS. HE SAID TO HIS FRIENDS "T he biggest step to financial freedom is the libration from d ebt"

CHAPTER

23

THE POWER OF ATTRACTION
"Much attracts much and little attracts little "

I f you find a wealthy man in Athens, he carries with hi m a charisma that makes him divine and admirable. T he very rich who knew this secret and understood it h ave used it countless of times upon the ignorant and even the educated to gain favors and positions in the society. W ealth in Athens is not about money but also power and po wer came from politics, sorcery, business, and religion, bec ause Athens practice democracy, the power was in the han ds of the people; the voted people in and out of seats and also voted for major decisions in the state. It was through t he power of democracy that Athenians voted for the death of Socrates and also whether to support the construction o f the Parthenon by Pericles or not; the people were the so urce of power and to be powerful in Athens, a man must n ot only just be wealthy or a hero in war but must also kno w how to win the heart of the people, for power lies not in wealth or positions but in the people. It was through this d emocracy by free voting among Athenians that Themistocl es the Athenian *strategoi* (word for an Athenian general or commander) was voted into exile and endangered his life i n the hands of the Spartans who tried to kill him, and so he had no other choice but to flee into the service of the ene mies he once fought against and won (the Persians) and th e Persian king Artaxerxes I, enrolled him as a governor ove r Magnesia. Themistocles at the end of his stay lost the po wer in the hands of the Athenians that he fought so hard f or and led to victory.

Prominent men in Athens began to find a secret way to wi n people's heart and so was BASILEUS, and until he discov ered it his wealth made no impact.

...

BASILEUS DECIDED TO ALSO REVEAL TO THEM ANOTHER S ECRET THAT MADE WEALTHY MEN IN ATHENS POWERFUL. HE SAID TO THEM:

"I thought that wealth was power until I saw where men o f power overshadowed the wealth of the very rich that ha d no power, it was like when the powerful tyrant Talys ban ished the 500 wealthiest citizens of Sybaris, they had wealt h but no power and power only came when a man is in pos ition and can command a force like the army. Talys was po werful because he was in position to command the armies of Sybaris to do as his heart pleases and whoever stands in his way was killed; the 500 wealthiest people who were no t in position and could not control power like Talys so they had to run for their lives. And ever since this event, men of wealth and substance began to use their wealth and influe nce to chase after power and positions, for with power the y could secure their wealth and have a say in the society.

ANTONIO: "How then can a man win the wealth of the peo ple since the majority of the power lies in the people and n ot in his hands?"

BASILEUS: "Well, from my experience, a man can win the people if he can attract them to himself and the best way i s to live an attractive life. A man must show gratitude to ev eryone and for everything he possesses, and as he desires power so must he desire service for power is buried under service, the number of people that can enjoy your service t ells how influential and powerful you can be; in a kingdom, the king is the most powerful because he serves everyone and influences everyone IN THE KINGDOM. You must be willing to volunteer in all things, when people come to you, treat them as nobles and make them feel very special, smile with them when necessary and create the time to listen to them"

BASILEUS THEN TOLD THEM OF A FRIEND HE MET IN CORINTH; HE WAS RICH, POWERFUL, AND HIGHLY RESPECTED.

"When I was in Corinth, I met a powerful merchant and I was impressed on how he handles issues. He talks little and often through silence, and focuses mainly on accomplishing task. If he has a task before him or something he wishes to do, he does not keep talking about it but sets out quietly to accomplish it and then presents to you the results, it is the results that people love and start talking about, so when he says "I will do it" his servants will leave happily for they could tie their hopes to his words because his word was his bond.

I also learnt a powerful way of attracting people and that is through gifts, he always had gifts kept for his visitors and close friends. When I visited him, he offered me Pearls, and I loved pearls, when the fabric seller visited him, he offered him the latest of fabrics, and then I knew that he not only gives gifts but also chooses his gifts wisely and gives to men the things they value and appreciate the most. So, I no longer give gifts at random, I give what the receiver values the most at that time and if he be hungry, I give him food to eat. Three things then have I learnt from this merchan t: Integrity of words, Accomplishments, and Gifts. People will follow you if they can trust you enough and benefit from you.

SO MY FRIENDS, MANY THINGS A MAN MUST DO TO ATTRACT PEOPLE TO HIM, AND ATHENS LOVE MEN WHO CAN LEAD AND BRING VICTORY AND GLORY TO THEM.

ANAKLETOS: "But Rich Basileus, why does the priest always insist of a life of gratitude? The last time we visited the Temple he enquired of us to show more gratitude when we deal with people"

ANTONIO: "Very true Basileus, he said that gratitude is a thing that the poor lacked so they become poorer by the day because they are ungrateful and do not see any reason to be grateful, all they see is the suffering that surrounds them and how unfair life has been but if only they could be more grateful for the little they have, more will come their way"

BASILEUS: "Yes my friends, the priest is very true in what he said to you and to been grateful makes a man humble and also powerful. See the politicians in Athens and how they deal with people, even if they dislike a person they would suppress that hatred and pretend to be happy and say all sort of nice words to him and even offer such a person exotic gifts in appreciation and when that person leaves their presence, he goes into the city and spread the good will of the politician and says the good things he had done. Now if th e politician can pretend to have a grateful heart and win su ch a number of people to himself, how much more a man who truly has a grateful heart, he will entice even the gods to his favor and draw into his life great abundance. The on e who has more attracts more and the one who has little a ttracts little."

AT THIS POINT BASILEUS THEN SAID TO THEM, "DO NOT F ORGET, PEOPLE ARE ONE OF YOUR GREATEST SOURCE OF POWER, THE MORE PEOPLE YOU CAN ATTRACT TO YOUR L IFE, THE MORE POWERFUL YOU WILL BECOME. USE GIFTS, GESTURES, ACHIEVEMENTS, GRATITUDE, AND LOYALTY TO ATTRACT OTHERS

CHAPTER

24

KNOW YOUR ENEMY
Your enemy is your breakthrough.

Your enemy is your breakthrough. Keep them closer.

Athens became great because of the enemies they could conquer. In the battle of Salamis around 480BC, Themistocles lead the Greek Ally armies with about 400 ships against the Persians led by Xerxes I with over 1000 ships. Although Eurybiades and the Spartans argued with Themistocles about fighting at salamis but rather moving from Salamis to Corinth where they could build city walls to protect them from the Persians but Themistocles was very convinced that the victory will be won at Salamis. He moved the other Greece-city-states to support him with ships and armies.

Now the Persians were very sure of victory over the Greeks, in fact lagend holds the Xarxes I built a throne at the sea shore to watch the battle and how the Greek armies will be defeated. Themistocles knew the desires of King Xarxes I and used the servant Sicinnus to lure the Persians who went out at night searching for the Greek army so they could strike them before down. The Persians were lured into the strait (a narrow passage of water connecting two sea or other large areas of water) and in the strait, the Persian large ships could neither maneuver and turn back, the Greek armies maximized this opportunity and used the sea and the strait to their advantage, although Artemisia (Xarxes female commander) warned Xarxes to wait until the Greeks surrender but he was too confident and sure of victory and so he sent over a thousand ship of armies and the Greeks def eated the Persians in the Battle of Salamis because THEY S TUDIED THE ENEMY, LURED HIM, MADE HIM FELT MORE P OWERFUL AND VICTORIOUS AND THEM CONQUERD HIM. with 371 ships under the command of Themistocles, the P ersian 1207 ships were defeated and this brought glory an d power to Athens after the first destruction of their city b y the Persians.

THE VICTORY OF GREECE AT THE BATTLE OF SALAMIS BECA ME THE BREAKTHROUGH FOR WESTERN CIVILIZTION AND THE GOLDEN AGE OF ATHENS.

*Spyglass Hill. The Molossian Naval Academy.www.molossia.org/milacademy/salamis.html

...

Making the most of enemies

An argument between Anakletos and some rival merchant s who have risen against his trade and have drawn most of his buyers to themselves. Anakletos was very worried as th is made his sales dropped down very rapidly so he went to see Basileus thinking that since Basileus was very influenti al he could do something on the issue "So you said the me rchants are trying to take over your customers?" "Yes my l ord, they are taking my buyers away from me and I am hel pless to what they are doing" "then you see them as enem ies?" "Yes I do, they are hindering my progress and I see t hem as a threat to my trade" "Hmmmm Anakletos, there i s something you must know to be a successful merchant" "what is it wise Basileus that I must know to be successful?

219

" "Well Anakletos, you must understand that your enemy i s not a threat but a source of wealth and power" "Source of wealth and power? How?" "Yes Anakletos, your enemy should not be seen as a threat but an advantage to achievi ng greatness, accumulating wealth and becoming powerful "

AND ANAKLETOS WAS REALLY AMAZED WITH WHAT BASIL EUS WAS SAYING FOR HE EXPECTED BASILEUS TO SEE THIN GS THE WAY HE SAW IT AND HOW EVERYONE THOUGHT A BOUT IT BUT HE APPROACHED THE MATTER DIFFERENTLY.

Instead of seeing the enemy as a threat, Basileus sees the enemy as an advantage and a source of achieving greatnes s.

"You see my friend, every enemy that comes your way co mes to either take from you or for you to take from him, if he conquers you, you will submit to him and everything yo u possess shall be his but if you overcome him, everything he has and come with shall be yours. Without enemies the re can be no transformation and development. Look at Ath ens, the land has become powerful because of its victory o ver the Persians and I have grown very wealthy. through th e making of armors and supplying of woods for ship makin g, why? The Athenians must prepare every hour against th e enemy, this day we are hearing of the greatness of the y oung Alexander the great, his power and wealth from a far distance because of his many victory over empires and wh en he conquered these empires, he toke over the cities an d the wealth in them, it was said that the great Philosophe r Aristotle had trained the young Alexander on military str ategy and equipped with the ability to understand his ene mies and employ strong military strategies to win his oppo nents, he uses their weakness to it advantage and what th ey lacked, he empowered himself with"

ANAKLETOS: "Does this mean I should just stand and watc h them without doing anything to protect myself against t hem?"

BASILEUS: "Of course No Anakletos, you have a great work to do and that is to understand your enemy, you are to stu dy every aspect of your enemy; what makes them stronger and powerful and what makes them weaker and timid, you should know the added advantage they have over you and if you cannot beat them in their strongest points then you bring up a strategy that will help you overcome them and until you learn how to overcome your enemies, they shall f orever dominate your wealth and power and enrich thems elves by taking from you. Every merchant knows that to be successful in sales he must acquire new skills to make him more higher there is no enough skill for greatness becaus e every level you arrive has a greater enemy waiting for yo u.

SO I SUGGEST MY FRIEND ANAKLETOS, DO NOT DISLIKE OR RUN AWAY FROM YOUR ENEMY AND COMPETITORS, SEE T HEM AS AN OPPORTUNITY FOR GREATER GOOD AND GLO RY, FOR EVERY ENEMY COMES WITH AN ABUNDANCE OF WEALTH AND POWER BEHIND HIM AND UNTIL YOU CONQ UER HIM, YOU CAN NEVER HAVE ACCESS TO THAT POWER

AND WEALTH.

And with these words, Anakletos saw his enemies from a d ifferent light and was even happy for having them because they showed to him the things that are missing in his busin ess and how much he must develop himself with new skill and business strategies in oreder to become successful in what he does.

IF A MAN HAS NO ENEMY, HE WOULD NOT APPRECIATE ST RENGHT AND HE WILL NO KNOW HOW WEAK HE HAD BEC OME OVER THE YEARS. THE ENEMY HAS COME TO EITHER I MPOVERISH YOU OR TO ENRICH YOU WITHOUT HIS KNOW ING.

CHAPTER

25

BUILD YOURSELF A SYSTEM

A system consists of the sum of cells, tissues, and organs.
He who can create a system has mastered the creation of
wealth

Today ANTINIO went to the Agora to buy some household goods for his wife and when he arrived, the place was very crowded with different traders buying and selling. He needed a good jewel and linen and when he was in the market place, he sighted one of Basileus servants trading jewels and he approached him

SERVANT: "My lord, the gods must be good today" ...AS HE SMILED AT ANTONIO COMING··· "What brought you to the Agora at this early hour of the morning?"

ANTONIO WALKED TO THE SERVANT WITH EXCITEMENT AND RESPONDED

"The old man must put a smile on someone, so how is business Mabri? I never knew your master had opened a new sale room in the Agora."

"O! Master it's no news, we have opened over a month now and not far from here is another new sale room manned by Tamza."

"Hmmm, I see, that is really nice. I never knew BASILEUS has two sales shop in the Agora" and Mabri interrupted "No Sir, Master has now 21 sales rooms in the Agora at different spots" "wow! 21? That is much how and when but we did not know"

"True Sir, Rich Master Basileus has made most of us his servants as heads over the shops in the Agora he believes tha t by having more locations for sales, he can acquire more p rofit from his business"

ANTONIO: "Yes it is true although I have not seen any mer chant in Athens owing so many locations as Basileus, altho ugh I was almost tempted to think its greed but I am seein g a different aspect of what you are talking about"

SERVANT: "O! NO my lord, it is not greed but a business st rategy, master does tell us that building a system and havi ng proper control over it is the best way of multiplying inc ome, in fact, he also has other locations in some of the Gre ece-city-states and hopes to build a stronger and better sy stem"

ANTONIO WAS SPEECHLESS AND HE SAT DOWN LISTENING TO THE SERVANT WHO HAS NOW BECOME SO EXPERIENC ED AND SKILLED IN THE BUSINESS AND ALL WHAT HE WAS TALKING ABOUT MADE ANTONIO TO SEE HOW SHALLOW THEY HAVE LIVED ALL THESE YEARS

ANTONIO: "So tell me Mabri, do you not think your maste r uses you unfairly?"

AND MABRI SMILED AND RESPONDED

MABRI: "No, master treats us well and we only feel very pr ivileged working under him, for example, he has given me f ull access to the goods in this shop and I do the business as mine for I also profit from every sale and there is no better labor in Athens that can pay a servant so well as what I no w do. I earn more than some of the free men of Athens for

Master had released unto my purse a percent of every sale "

ANTONIO: "Hmmm, that is good I must say Mabri, although I came for a nice piece of jewel but you have empowered me with something more valuable than a jewel and I feel so privileged meeting you today"

SERVANT: "The privilege is mine my lord" AND HE SMILED

ANTONIO: "Tell me then, for I see that the goods in your store are very much, how do you dispose them so easily?" ANTONIO ASKED THIS QUESTION BECAUSE THE FEW TIME HE HAD STOOD THERE, SOME PEOPLE CAME TO BUY THE GOODS IN BULK FROM MABRI

MABRI: "My Lord, the business is very simple; Master has taught us so well on how to handle every part of the trade. You see the men that came to buy in large quantities?" and he replied "yes I do" "well, they work under me, master gets the goods straight from the producers and hands it over to us, and we add a little profit on it before handing it to the buyers, some buyers who seek to work under master's name are considered and treated like us but a certain percentage will go to master at the end of their trade for they are now partners with him and those goods that master produces on his own like the armor and the potteries he sells to them at a producers price and they market it for him and bring to him more buyers and people who wish to open more sale rooms in different parts of Greece.

AND SO DID ANTONIO SAT DOWN UNDER THE GREAT LESS
ONS OF MABRI AND WHEN HE WENT HOME THAT DAY, HE
LOOKED AT HIS SERVANTS AND HIS BUSINESS AND SAW H
OW UNWISE HE HAD BECOME···AND SO IT ENDED THAT A
NTONIO DECIDED TO EXPAND HIS BUSINESS

The Parable Of The Pipeline (Adapted from Burke Hedges book on the parable of the pipeline)

Once upon a time long, long ago, two ambitious young cousins named Pablo and Bruno lived side by side in a small Italian village. The young men were best buddies, and big dreamers. They would talk endlessly about how someday, someway, they would become the richest men in the village. They were both bright and hard working. All they needed was an opportunity.

One day that opportunity arrived. The village decided to hire two men to carry water from a nearby river to a cistern in the town square. The job went to Pablo and Bruno. Each man grabbed two buckets and headed to the river. By the end of the day, they had filled the town cistern to the brim. The village elder paid them one penny for each bucket of water.

"This is our dream come true!" Shouted Bruno. "I can't believe our good fortune."

But Pablo wasn't so sure.

His back ached and his hands were blistered from carrying the heavy buckets. He dreaded getting up and going to work the next morning. He vowed to think of a better way to get the water from the river to the village.

Pablo The Pipeline Man:
"Bruno, I have a plan," Pablo said the next morning as they grabbed their buckets and headed for the river. "Instead of lugging buckets back and forth for pennies a day, let's build a pipeline from the village to the river."
Bruno stopped dead in his tracks.
"A pipeline! Whoever heard of such a thing?" Bruno shouted. "We've got a great job, Pablo. I can carry 100 buckets a day. At a penny a bucket that's a dollar a day! I'm rich!. By the end of the week, I can buy a new pair of shoes. By the end of the month a cow. By the end of six months I can buy a new hut. We have the best job in town. We have weekends off and two weeks paid vacation every year. We're set for life! Get out of here with your pipeline."
But Pablo was not easily discouraged. He patiently explained the pipeline plan to his best friend. Pablo would work part of the day carrying buckets, and part of the day and weekends building his pipeline.
He knew it would be hard work digging a ditch in the rocky soil. Because he was paid by the bucket, he knew his income would drop. He also knew it might take a year or two before his pipeline would pay off. But Pablo believed in his dream and he went to work.

Bruno and the rest of the villagers began mocking Pablo, calling him "Pablo The Pipeline Man." Bruno, who was earning almost twice the money as Pablo, flaunted his new purchases. He bought a donkey outfitted with a new leather saddle, which he kept parked outside his new two-story hut. He bought flashy clothes and fancy meals at the inn. The villagers called him Mr. Bruno, and they cheered when he bought rounds at the tavern and laughed loudly at his jokes.

Small Actions Equal Big Results:

While Bruno lay in his hammock on evenings and weekends, Pablo kept digging his pipeline. The first few months Pablo didn't have much to show for his efforts.

The work was hard, even harder than Bruno's because Pablo was working evenings and weekends too.

But Pablo kept reminding himself that tomorrow's dreams are built on today's sacrifices. Day by day he dug, inch by inch.

Inches turned into one foot........... then ten feet............ then 20............. then 100.

"Short-term pain equals long-term gain," he reminded himself as he stumbled into his hut after another exhausting day's work. "In time my reward will exceed my efforts," he thought.

"Keep your eyes on the prize," he kept thinking as he drifted off to sleep with the sounds of laughter from the village tavern in the background.

The Tables Are Turned:

Days turned into months. One day Pablo realized his pipeline was half-way finished, which meant he only had to walk half as far to fill his buckets! Pablo used the extra time to work on his pipeline.

During his rest breaks, Pablo watched his old friend Bruno lug buckets. Bruno's shoulders were more stooped than ever. He was hunched in pain, his steps slowed by the daily grind. Bruno was angry and sullen, resenting the fact that he was doomed to carry buckets, day in, day out, for the rest of his life.

He began to spend less time in his hammock and more time in the tavern. When the tavern's patrons saw Bruno coming they'd whisper, "Here comes Bruno the Bucket Man," and they giggle when the town drunk mimicked Bruno's stooped posture and shuffling gait. Bruno didn't buy rounds or tell jokes anymore, preferring to sit alone in a dark corner surrounded by empty bottles.

Finally Pablo's big day arrived, his pipeline was complete! The villagers crowded around as the water gushed from the pipeline into the village cistern! Now that the village had a steady supply of fresh water, people from around the countryside moved into the village and the village prospered.

Once the pipeline was complete, Pablo didn't have to carry buckets anymore. The water flowed whether he worked or not. It flowed while he ate. It flowed while he slept. It flowed on weekends while he played. The more the water flowed into the village, the more money flowed into Pablo's pockets!

Pablo the Pipeline Man became known as Pablo the Miracle Maker. But Pablo understood what he did wasn't a miracle. It was merely the first stage of a big, big dream. You see, Pablo had bigger plans. Pablo planned on building pipelines all over the world!.

Recruiting His Friend To Help:

The pipeline drove "Bruno The Bucket Man" out of business, and it pained Pablo to see his old friend begging for drinks at the tavern. So, Pablo arranged a meeting with his old friend.

"Bruno, I've come here to ask you for your help." Bruno straightened his stooped shoulders, and his dark eyes narrowed to a squint. "Don't mock me," Bruno hissed.

"I haven't come here to gloat," said Pablo. "I've come here to offer you a great business opportunity. It took me more than two years before my first pipeline was complete. But I've learned a lot during those two years. I know what tools to use now, and where to dig. I know where to lay the pipe. I kept notes as I went along so now I have a system that will allow me to build another pipeline in less time.......... then another..........then another.

I could build a pipeline a year by myself, but what I plan on doing is teach you how to build a pipeline, then have you teach others and have them teach others.

"Just think, we could make a small percentage of every gallon of water that goes through those pipelines."

Bruno finally saw the big picture. They shook hands and hugged like old friends.

Pipeline Dreams In A Bucket-Carrying World:

Years passed. Their world pipelines were pumping millions of dollars into their bank accounts. Sometimes on their trips through the countryside, Pablo and Bruno would pass villagers from other villages carrying buckets.

The friends would pull over and tell them their story and offer to help them build a pipeline. But sadly, most bucket carriers would hastily dismiss the notion.

"I don't have the time."

"My friend told me he knew a friend who's uncle's best friend tried to build a pipeline and failed."

"Only the ones who get in early make money on a pipeline."

"I've carried buckets my whole life, I'll stick to what I know."

"I know people who lost money in a pipeline scam."

Both men resigned themselves to the fact they lived in a world with a bucket-carrying mentality............. and only a very small percentage of people would ever see the vision.

CHAPTER

26

GAIN POSITIONS

"It is not titles that honor men, but men that honor titles"

Niccolo Machiavelli

Today, PATIOS was at the PIRAEUS trying to clear his goods but he had challenges with the men in charge, they will not allow him to take his goods until he has the seal of the Grain Master, and he had no idea who the grain master was, so he asked how he can meet with the grain master and he was given the address of the Grain Master's office in the Bouleuterion. Patios left instantly in a rush so he could get his goods cleared that same day.

On his arrival at the Bouleuterion, he enquired of the Grain Master's office and was shown, on entering the office, Patios was shocked to find out that the Grain Master was Basileus himself.

PATIOS in a state of surprise greeted: "Good day Master Sir"

AND BASILEUS MET HIM WITH A GREAT SMILE

BASILEUS: "Good day Patios, you are welcome, how did you find your way down here?"

PATIOS: "O great Basileus, I was directed here from the Piraeus to come see the Grain Master and obtain his seal of approval before I can take my goods from the port"

BASILEUS: "Oh! I see, then you are much welcomed"

PATIOS: "But I never knew you were given such a great position Basileus, and I wonder if it is not a burden unto you for you have many businesses to look after"

BASILEUS: "Hmmm, young Patios, well it is not a burden b ut a privilege to serve as Athenian Grain Master, and I visit this very office just once in a week to put my seal on the va rious request, so I think you are fortunate seeing me today . For most times I am not here myself"

PATIOS: "I actually taught that such offices as the Grain M aster is acquired only by the politicians of the city for it is a powerful position on which Athens trade lies upon"

BASILEUS: "Very true Patios, and today I shall tell you som ething that many merchant take for granted for they think having money is all that they need to be influential in Athe ns until a certain problem arises where they must submit u nto men and women in position and power

You see, THE MOMENT I KNEW THAT WEALTH IS NOT PO WER I SOUGHT AFTER THEM DIFFERENTLY SO I CAN USE T HEM DEPENDENTLY. I saw that with money a man has influ ence but with power he has authority and can command; I saw that money brings admiration but power instill revere nce, sometimes fear, and respect. A man may be wealthy a nd not respected but he cannot be powerful without com manding respect and reverence. So I said to myself, where are the places that power dwells and finds shelter in? And I discovered three places; I found power in the temple of t he gods, the service of the priest and in the hands of sorce rers; secondly, I found power in the seat of kings and the p oliticians; and lastly, I found power in the hands of military men of war and valor

Then I sought within myself and discovered that there was a greater power within me which I had possessed even bef ore the first owl coin came to my purse and that power wa s of the wisdom which I had first acquired. This wisdom wa s the ultimate power, for it helps a man to command every seat of power he occupies and the wise man seeks first po wer before wealth.

PATIOS: "So rich Basileus, do you now say that wealth is n ot power and that very rich man should also be powerful? "

BASILEUS: "Men do think that wealth is power, but I have said to you Patios that wealth is not power and if a rich ma n wants to secure his wealth or have a say in the decision making of his Nation, he must be powerful, he must be abl e to command but so unfortunate are many who after the y acquired wealth confuse it for power, in fact, a man shou ld acquire power first so he can manage his wealth with it, such power comes from wisdom, skills, talents, abilities, an d most importantly positions. Power needs a position to m anifest. Today you need a seal to clear your goods, and tha t seal is under my control, nothing comes in and goes out o f Athens without my seal, and because of my position here in Athens, my goods are secured and so is my wealth, I hav e access to many people and things in Athens.

So it is good to attain power Patios, it will help you in a lot of matters concerning wealth; you should devote your tim e to voluntary works and when you are required for a posit ion, you should not shy away from responsibilities, for it is in these that power lies···

Now let me have your papers so I can put my seal on them
"

AND PATIOS HANDED HIM THE PAPERS FOR BASILEUS TO PUT HIS SEAL

BASILEUS: "So tell Patios, what do you know of Athens firs t Lady Aspasia?"

PATIOS: "That she is an intelligent hetaera"

"And what else?" asked Basileus, "She is from Miletus and became wealthy by been a companion of Pericles"

BASILEUS: "You've spoken rightly, but Aspasia was a much more different kind of woman who display high intellectua l prowess unlike other educated hetaerae, as a little girl sh e was handed over to be of service in the Temple of Aphro dite and after her years of service, she left for Athens wher e she started up her own business and managed a brothel also, one thing made Aspasia stand out and that is; she wa s outspoken and could debate intelligently and always win on her part, she was both smart and cunning and in few ye ars gained so much connection with most of the citizens of Athens.

They say that her beauty and prowess were irresistible tha t the Commander of Athens, Pericles could not help but ha ve her as his companion, he wished to marry her but Athe nian law does not permit citizens to get married to non citi zens, rumors also went that Aspasia was the hand behind most of Pericles speeches, decisions and judgments in Ath ens, although women were not permitted in Athens public life but Aspasia made her way through and became power ful through her companion Pericles whom she bore a son t o and also named him Pericles after his father.

Do you know why I share this with you?"

PATIOS: "NO RICH Basileus"

BASILEUS: "Well, that you may know that there is power in every position that a man occupies. Although Aspasia was not a citizen of Athens but she was able to influences Athe ns Public life and made crucial decisions through her husba nd. Her strength came from not just her beauty but her int elligence, she was also friend to most of Athenians philoso phers and was wise in handling issues; this wisdom was he r source of power and it attracted the most powerful man i n Athens, Pericles and made him submit to her every desir e. Her position as a companion of Pericles empowered her far beyond any woman in Athens and with it she also accu mulated great wealth."

THEN HE HANDED THE SEALED DOCUMENT TO PATIOS AN D SAID, "SO, Hurry up young merchant and go clear your g oods, but when you are back home and have rested, you s hould give a thought of what we have discussed unless you do wish coming always to get a seal for the clearance of yo ur goods" AND BASILEUS GAVE HIM A SMILE. PATIOS COLL ECTED THE PAPER WITH GREAT APPRECIATION TO BASILE

US.

PATIOS: "I am so grateful for all you have spoken to me thi s day, I see that the gods have made me fortunate knowin g you and learning from your wisdom"

AND SO HE LEFT THAT DAY WITH MUCH THOUGHT ON PO WER AND ITS ACQUISITION

STAY HAPPY

CHAPTER

27

THE EVIDENCE

Results speaks better than actions and louder than words

I N A WEEK FROM NOW, PATIOS WILL BE GETTING MARRIED.

After been under the guidance of Basileus for 12 years now, Patios had grown into one of Athens most wealthiest and powerful merchants. When he came to Basileus with his friends he was just a common trader in the Agora and had no shop to his name, he sold pearls on the street like any other young merchant aspiring for a breakthrough; he made not up to 2 drachma a day and lived most of his life on the streets.

Fortune met him at age 21 on that very day he decided to go with the group that chose to see THE RICHEST MERCHANT IN GREECE and to ask him about of the secret to his riches. PATIOS was a very young at that time and could not afford school because he was orphaned and had to start life on his own; he wanted to lead a responsible life and not steal or cheat to live, so he went to learn trade among the merchants of Athens. On that day, he went along with both ANTONIO and ANAKLETOS to see BASILEUS, The Richest Merchant in Greece to enquire from him how to accumulate wealth.

From that time till now, it has been 12 solid years under the mentorship of the Rich Basileus and today, PATIOS has become an independent merchant rich enough to also teach others who are interested on the path to prosperity. His life has become a living prove of what the influence of The Richest Merchant of Greece could be after 12 years of mentorship.

PATIOS now has four big ships to his name that travel to distant lands to bring the best of pearls, jewels, linen, perfumes, spices, and grains to Athens and also transport potteries from Athens to other cities. He also owns seven shops in the Agora and a luxurious house to live in, he built inns for travelers and houses for rent, and he also deals with the silver mined in Athens.

Today, just like the first luxurious Birthday PATIOS and his two friends went in the house of BASILEUS, PATIOS could today use his excess profit to celebrate such a birthday for himself; with the help of BASILEUS and the generous and loving heart of PATIOS, he was able to attain a powerful position in Athens as one of the advisers of the Athenian leader on commerce.

Although patios has achieved so much in a little time but has one more thing left which is marriage, and fortunate enough he has found himself a lovely young lady to wife and the wedding is scheduled in a week time.

...

ANTONIO has in 12 years accumulated so much than he imagined, he has built for himself a powerful network of businesses across Athens and trained his servants to head different aspects of his trade. He joined BASILEUS in the making of Armors and potteries for export; he also went into different business investment and has acquired more slaves to himself which he trains and treats like his business partners.

He also assists BASILEUS in the monitoring of trade in Athens and built different houses for rent, he invested his income into Athenian art and tragic plays for during this time, Athens became the center of Arts and entertainment. People rush into the theaters at any cost to be entertained and ANTONIO became one of the largest investors in the entertainment sector of Athens. His wealth grew greatly and so was his power and influence.

He also trained his children in the business and taught them how to generate wealth, maintain it and also teach others.

...

ANAKLETOS on the other hand became a master genius in business deals; he takes everyone as a potential client be it friends or enemies. He has mastered how to win and draw the wealth of his competitors. He buys the crumbling trade of merchants and transforms it into a huge success. Every merchant in Athens feared Anakletos for his business acumen, with this ability, he has been able to own 16 shops in the Agora, build a great mansion unto himself and owns a large number of camels, sheep, cattle, and goats.

He was made a representative of Athenian trade in foreign cities and countries due to his ability to negotiate every trade and win at all bargains. He won many contracts of the leaders of Athens. He also invested in the sports of Greece (The Olympics dedicated to the god Zeus); this made him a lot of money and so did he increased everyday in his riches.

...

TODAY THE THREE MEN DECIDED TO HOST THE RICH BASILEUS TO A LUXURIOUS DINNER IN ONE OF ANTONIOS LUXURIOS INNS

The inn was booked for the whole evening and everything was arranged with great luxury, servants bringing in exotic dishes from different cities, and drinks. BASILEUS was amazed at the sight of the inn and the beauty it displays, the table was well set with great dishes and both ANTONIO and ANAKLETOS were on the standing as PATIOS walked the Rich Basileus to the table. The three sat down with great joy and respect for their master who had taught and mentored them for 12 good years.

BASILEUS: "This is very impressive gentle men, you shouldn't have stressed yourself this hard for an old man like me" AND HE SMILED

ANTONIO: "Rich Basileus, it is but a privilege to host you here at last, it has been our dream ever since we start meeting with you and especially the day you told us of the parable of the acres of diamonds and before you started, you said you look forward to having a dinner in our place someday and today fulfills those words after 12 years learning from you"

ANAKLETOS: "Very true Basileus, you gave us something we could never have had if we depended on ourselves, today we are a product of that one decision to meet you after that argument at the Agora where we divided with Lycus and his group in search of riches and honor, today here I am a totally different man from who I use to be 12 years ago"

PATIOS: "I own my success to your mentorship Rich Basileus, and every lesson I learnt transformed itself into great wealth and abundance, with your help I also grew in power and outran men of my age. After 12 solid years with you, I shall never regret any days of it for those years are my greatest treasures on earth"

BASILEUS WAS VERY MOVED WITH THEIR WORDS AND APPRECIATED THE GREAT TRANSFORMATION THEY HAD UNDERGONE WITH HIM UNDER A PERIOD OF 12 YEARS... AND HE LOOKED AT EACH OF THEM AND NOW ASKED

"So tell me today, am I monopolist?" And they all laughed and responded "Of course No Rich Basileus, it is that you understood that many lacked and that understanding made you a ruler over them all"

HE WAS PLEASED WITH THEIR ANSWERS AND THEN FUTHER ASKED

"Now that you've all grown this rich, will there still be enough wealth to go round for the other merchants in Athens?"

And they all chorused "There is enough wealth for everyone!" and PATIOS added that, "One man's abundance is not a reason for another man's impoverishment, whoever wants to be rich can be rich"

AND THEY ALL TOAST TO THE GOOD LIFE IN FRONT OF THEM

BASILEUS: "Least I forget, Patios, how is your wedding plan going?"

PATIOS: "Very great my Lord, it is in a week time and I shall be honored to have you as the master of the ceremony"

AND THEY ALL MADE A JOKE OF EVERYTHING AND HAD A WONDERFFUL DINNER TOGETHER

CHAPTER

28

BUILDING A FAMILY
After all, it is family that counts the most

TODAY IS PATIOS WEDDING DAY AND THE WHOLE OF ATHENS KNEW THAT SOMETHING UNIQUE IS HAPPENING IN ATHENS

Marriages in Athens are quite different from other cities or Nations as the families involved looked out mainly for personal interest and needs. Most of the marriages were arranged by the parents and in some cases, the bride and the groom may have never known each other until that day of the wedding. The father of the bride marries out his daughter to a man he sees fit and can be of value to him and to such a man, a hands over his daughter with a dowry to her husband.

After the different rituals, the woman is then welcomed to her husband's house and begins to worship the gods of her husband, as he is now her new lord and master. Although a man can marry more than one wife if he so wishes but mainly, the law suggests one wife for one man but that he can also have concubines and mistresses if he so wishes, but such concubines are not recognized as his wives, the law will only recognize the woman he married.

And also, Athenian Citizens are forbidden by law to marry outsiders (non-citizens), that was why the great leader Pericles could not take Aspasia as his legal wife because she was not a citizen of Athens, he made her his companion but treated her as equal as he would treat a wife.

...

PATIOS was fortunate that the lady he wished to marry was the lady he fell in love with, he actually had a Lady at his early start of life but because he had no money to look after her, she left him for another man who she feels has enough money. These were some of the reasons that made PATIOS toke the bold step of getting rich at all cost, he could not really maintain a good relationship because of his lean purse but along the way, he met this lady who was very jovial and free to be with and she loved him without thinking much of his money, and so did their relationship grew for six good years and when PATIOS finally became so rich, there was no better woman to spent the rest of his life with than the funny and straight forward lady he had spent six years of his life with, a lady who watched him as he moved from his rags to riches.

THE ACROPOLIS WAS FILLED WITH SO MUCH PEOPLE AND GREAT PERSONALITIES. BASILEUS, ANTONIO, AND ANAKLETOS WERE ALL SITTED ALONG SIDE SOME OF ATHENS TOP SENATORS AND THE LEADER HIMSELF.

BASILEUS was the master of the ceremony and took charge of most of the marital expense, ANTONIO and ANAKLETOS took charge of the gifts, food and drinks. The wedding was a talk about in town as Athens had never witness such a wedding that so much was spent and people had enough food and gifts to go home with. Every young lady in Athens wished they had PATIOS as a husband. They wedding were graced by influential and power people from all works of life and cities. It was a happy day for PATIOS and his newly wedded wife. THE

CITY CALLED THE BRIDES FATHER A MOST FORTUNATE MAN FOR ALL HIS NEEDS WILL BE TAKEN GOOD CARE OF AND HE SHALL PROFIT GREATLY.

...

AFTER THEIR "HONEY MOON", PATIOS VISITED BASILEUS TO SHOW HIS APPRECIATION

BASILEUS: "my pleasure PATIOS, but you must not forget that a good man in the public is first know at home, if you cannot manage your home, you will not be able to manage the public. I will say that your wife is fortunate getting married to you but you must also show her the way to be a woman of independence and great skill; you must fill her with wisdom and discipline and teach her how to make money and not fully depend on your wealth alone. This is the great mistake many rich men do, they deny their wives the freedom to acquire skills that can enrich them and when they die, both the wife and her children burn the riches away.

But if a woman is trained on how to generate and maintain wealth, she would never be impoverished even when her husband's wealth is taken away from her."

PATIOS: "But rich Basileus are not women deprived of public responsibilities in Athens?"

BASILEUS: "Yes they are but it no one prevents a man from empowering his wife. Do not follow the path of men who see their wives as another possession in the house and keep them locked from life. Do not use marriage to bind her from life but use it to empower her so that she can be a better part of you in all dealings and ensure that you draft a will concerning everything you possess, do not wait until you grow old or about to die before you decide what inheritance goes to everyone that matters to your life.

Create a time and see the law giver tomorrow so you can make a will statement of what you posses, you may travel someday and not return or sleep tomorrow and not wake up to life again, no man knows when death will come, so you must prepare for it when you are alive so that your family and wealth will not crumble into pieces when you are no more"

THESE WORDS PIERCED PATIOS AS HE THOUGHT DEEPLY OF WHAT BASILEUS WAS SAYING

PATIOS: "I am very grateful Master; I shall bid to your every word. I do appreciate all that you have done for me and I say thank you once more."

AND HE LEFT THAT DAY WITH AN ADVICE THAT WILL HELP HIS LIFE AND HIS NEW FAMILY

CHAPTER

29

GIVE BACK TO THE COMMUNITY
Better to give than to receive

P ATIOS had become very rich that he decided to retire four years after his wedding and at the age of 37, he has no reason to worry about money or work for someone to make money, he only sat down in his luxurious house and enjoys a happy home with travelling from one city and nation to another, so also ANTONIO and ANAKLETOS although they still had responsibilities for the state of Athens and their expertise was requested when needed.

After making so much wealth in their lifetime, each of them started executing works for the people and city of Athens.

PATIOS who was not privileged to gain a formal education when he was young decided to sponsor children and teenagers who wanted to gain formal education. He also equipped them with the necessary materials needed to have a comfortable learning. He also built more classrooms for the Academy of Athens and made donations to the school. And for the women of Athens, Patios build a skill center where most women could acquire the basic skills to start a normal life and ease the financial burden upon their husbands

ANAKLETOS embarked on building an orphanage home for the less privileged, he gave out money to the city physicians for proper health care of citizens who were not buoyant enough to pay their charges. He also distributes food especially in times of occasions and festivals and also contributed money to the Olympics and helped channeled water to communities that were lacking.

ANTONIO helped in furnishing part of the temples in Athens and with the help of the other friends; they also built a place for prayers. He gave out some of his houses out for free to those who lived in it, and contributed a percentage of his wealth to the Athenian Army so that the City of Athens s could be strengthened.

THE THREE MEN WHO HAVE NOW BECOME SOME OF ATHENS TOP MEN BOTH IN TRADE AND POLITICS DECIDED TO GIVE OUT A PERCENTAGE OF THEIR WEALTH BACK TO THE COMMUNITY IN ORDER TO HELP THE LESS PRIVILEGE ONES

They also gave advice freely unto anyone who came to them or the matters of wealth and other burdens of life and he who sought to borrow from them they deny not and most times gave freely. And they did all these with great love and happiness in their hearts, they gave willingly and not in compulsion or trying to impress the community but in order to touch lives and solve problems that others see and neglect.

The people of Athens remained very grateful to such men and most especially their teacher and mentor BASILEUS who have lived a truly successful man and were able to bring up men who could be like him and also share their riches.

ANTONIO, ANAKLETOS AND PATIOS gained the life they desired and remained grateful to BASILEUS for what he had done to them all throughout the years.

CHAPTER

30

DIE RICH

He is the richest that dies fulfilled

ANTONIO was attending to some matters at the Agora when a servant rushed to him in utter despair and confusion and announced to him the dead of Rich Basileus some few minutes ago. ANTONIO became very worried and sent servants immediately to contact ANAKLETOS and PATIOS and informed them of the news.

...

BASILEUS had lived a very rich life although lived part of his youthful age as a slave but later gained freedom through the help of the priest who set his life of fortune on course. He died at the age of 96 leaving a wife and six children; his life was a blessing to many who related with him especially now Athens three wealthiest men. He did so much for the people and was loved by many and also envied by most.

He neither was sick nor killed but slept peacefully in the night and never woke up again to see the light of the morning. Those who beheld his corpse said he died a happy death for his continence was as peaceful as ever.

...

A WEEK BEFORE HIS DEAD

BASILEUS: "So my lord have you amended the will I asked you to?"

LAWYER: "Yes Master Basileus, I have done all that you asked. I separated the various properties of your wife from that of your children and also the once for your family, relatives, and the public"

BASILEUS: "That is good, please do keep it safe and do as I have told you when I am no more"

LAWYER: "Yes my Lord"

RICH BASILEUS calls upon the Law giver of the City four times in a year to go through his will and adds or removes whatever he desired for as the day goes by, his wealth accumulated greatly. A week before his death, he called upon the law giver to review his will and made the necessary changes needed.

In his life time, he had trained both his wife and kid on how to manage every section of his business and also men like Antonio, Anakletos, and Patios. He built different houses under the names of his wife and children and has allocated different business to them. He made a protective law against his family members taking over his possession from his wife and children. He equipped his wife with so much skill and wisdom that she could properly start up life on her own and regenerate wealth for herself without necessarily depending on his possessions.

He also handed his children under the custody of Antonio, Anakletos, and Patios who would be like father unto them and over see the management of the properties. All these he did and addressed every bit of his life before his dead.

...

THE HOUSE OF BASILEUS WAS FILLED WITH PEOPLE CRYING FOR THE LOST OF A GREAT AND WEALTHY MAN

Dignitaries from across nations began flocking into Athens to witness if what they heard was true. And so it was that the Rich Basileus slept without waking up to the light of life anymore. It was a heavy moment for the three friends and disciples of BASILEUS but at the same time they did not worry too much for Basileus had lived a well aged and prosperous life and there was nothing to worry about after his dead for he owed no man and built for himself a great name beyond his death.

It was a huge burial ceremony for BASILEUS and Antonio, Anakletos, and Patios paid for every expense and dedicated a sculpture to BASILEUS and also a building for the equipping of youths who aspire to find the purpose and meaning of life and also walk in the path of prosperity.

...

After a week of BASILEUS dead, the city lawyer brought his family together and read out the will unto them and handed over the children to Antonio, Anakletos, and Basileus so they could be mentored in the trade of the merchants and also the acquisition of power.

NO MAN IS SAID TO BE FORTUNATE UNTIL HIS DEATH

- GREEK PROVERB

CHAPTER

31

LIVING BEYOND THE GRAVES
Even the grave cannot hold back the deeds of a good man

T hey say, "A man may die but a good name lives beyond the grave"

THE NAME BASILEUS left the graves unto the lips and hearts of men and was carried from generations to generations. Kings, commanders, Merchants, and Heroes were honored by the name BASILEUS in the Greek empire which means King and Lord.

ANTONIO, ANAKLETOS, and PATIOS went on to lead a glorious life and devoted their time to teach others on THE WISDOM OF BASILEUS and the path to wealth, abundance, and power. These men by their teachings made great disciples who prospered in Athens and made the city greater. Athens, the favorite city of the gods enjoyed great prosperity and abundance before its fall around 322BC, and from it the world was blessed with some of the wisest men on earth whose philosophy, strength, and skills brought about the great civilization we now enjoy today. The principles of wealth used during the times of BASILEUS are same principles used today with modification due to the advancement of the world but the principles and laws of getting rich and prosperous in life still remains the same from generation to generation and will still produce same result as it always use to, in the end, a man in all his getting should also get riches if he can, he should be powerful, and learn to stay happy. This was the story of THE RICHEST MERCHANT IN GREECE.

THE END

To publish and distribute this material in print please contact the author or amazon.com

www.ingramcontent.com/pod-product-compliance
Lightning Source LLC
Chambersburg PA
CBHW021421170526
45164CB00001B/48